FAITH FAMILY
and
Franchise

13 Lessons for Couples to Create a Heart-Centered Business

Clinton *and* DeAnna Lewis

Christian Living Books, Inc.
Largo, MD

ISBN 9781562293871

Christian Living Books, Inc.
P. O. Box 7584
Largo, MD 20792
christianlivingbooks.com
We bring your dreams to fruition.

ENDORSEMENTS

It is with extreme delight and joy that I endorse your book which was written to help up-and-coming entrepreneurs. God has blessed you for your faithfulness to your children, family, and church. This faithfulness shows in the success of your businesses and the diligent effort you both make as a team. I am proud to see how you have allowed God to lead and guide you one step at a time. Your success was achieved after failure and mistakes. To new entrepreneurs, please read this book and *do not* give up. God bless you is my prayer!

Bishop Howard A. Swancy
Peace Apostolic Church
Carson, CA

The Lewises passionately and candidly invite the reader into their world with these valuable life lessons. This power couple is sharing the blueprint to success with the world. This book will teach you how to strategically align your financial affairs, build an empire of generational wealth, and keep God as the center and source of all things. As friends for over thirty years, we have witnessed God transform their lives as a testament to others that hard work, dedication, and prayer is the primary foundation for success. We are confident that you will be encouraged and equipped with essential wisdom to also get your life in divine order. Their mandate is to leave an uncommon contribution in the earth realm with this tool.

Bishop Vernon R. Kemp
Greater Harvest Christian Center
Lady Vicki Kemp
Bestselling author of *Better than Yesterday*

Your honesty and transparency will impact so many readers' lives. Many of us are not ready to share the struggles of our lives. That might be due to embarrassment or shame. Perhaps we are not really ready to be honest with ourselves. We sometimes think we are the only ones going through a particular trial. So, thank you for being open and honest. You are a true blessing, not because of your success or philanthropic spirit, but because of your willingness to share your journey. This book will touch, encourage, and empower all of those around you just as your friendship has done throughout the years. We love you both!

Brandon Shelton
Nat'l Division Director of Commonwealth Spirit Health
Regina Shelton
Auto Claims Specialist

This is a must-read for anyone who dares to dream big. This inspiring couple strategically addresses the one thing often left out of most African American conversations – generational wealth! With faith as their backbone, they take us on their incredible journey to success. This guide is a guarantee that no family is left behind. It is a step-wise plan to create generational wealth as franchise owners.

Dennis Schaffer, Principal
Angel Schaffer, MD

We count it an *honor* and a *privilege* to endorse this new book. If you are looking for a publication that will give you the nuts and bolts and/or the blueprint for building successful businesses, this book is for you! For over 26 years, we have shared the same apostolic faith as Clint and Deanna. During this time, we have become "family" and "co-franchisees" of one of their numerous franchises. We have observed, firsthand, the grind, hustle, sweat, tears, growth, and success they shared in this book. Read it. Digest it, and make a plan. You will be blessed by it!

Kevin Dobson, Franchisee
Tamara Williams-Dobson, Author, Franchisee
Fatburger, Glendora, CA
Dobson Christian Preschool and Childcare, Eastvale, CA

CONTENTS

INTRODUCTION

L ife can be challenging, whether you are given the right tools for success or not. In fact, having the tools but not knowing how to use them presents as much of a challenge as not having them at all. Not to mention, not everyone has been given the keys to success. Unfortunately, the majority of people don't have the tools, knowledge, or connections they need. Does this mean only a few can live the American Dream while the others are stuck without the resources to figure it out? We don't think so! We believe you can find the right tools, get proper guidance, and figure out the dream you were gifted with to build your successful life.

Who are we? Meet DeAnna and Clint Lewis. We're some of those folks who were not born with connections, keys, or resources but were able to figure them out and succeed! We're also a couple dedicated to making sure others understand how to get what they want in a productive and efficient manner.

Faith, Family, and Franchise is one of the tools we have created to help you with that understanding. This book is our gift to you. We have worked for many years building successful businesses. In the process, the failures, tears, and disappointments have been stepping stones toward our success. Through it all, we realized this wasn't just the building of businesses for our gratification, but it is our ministry. You might say it's a calling. This ministry we share will allow you to take a virtual ride on the rollercoaster of our lives. You don't have to experience the same scary ride we did. In this book, you will see the good, the bad, the ugly, and the triumphs.

Our success didn't happen overnight. We lost many material things during our faith test, but we pushed through and passed with flying colors. When people meet us, they see the final product, but what's important to understand is the journey. The journey is where the rubber meets the road. Who you are traveling with is just as important as getting to your destination. In fact, who you travel with – mentors, partners, friends, and foes – will determine whether you even reach your goals.

For years, we have discussed writing a book that will help our community build successful businesses. We especially wanted to help couples because there's nothing better than having a partner who's really in it *with* you. We searched for books written by couples that focused on building wealth as a team heading multiple businesses. To our surprise, not many existed. Of course, there were the typical ministry books, cookbooks, and even home improvement books, but we couldn't find books on how to build a successful business with your spouse.

DEANNA

I was surprised. I just knew I would find what I was looking for in the bookstore but not one book existed. I couldn't believe it. I called Clint right away and said, "Babe, you're not gonna believe this." Of course, he was in work mode, but I talked his ear off about how we needed to write our book for the masses. We had to tell our story so people would stop being afraid of building businesses.

Entrepreneurship can be intimidating. I know that. However, I also know that if you stick to it, focus on God's plan, and persevere, you can do it. Some of us give up too fast. That's not going to build wealth. You must seriously go into prayer, use the tools in this book, and break down the walls of fear before moving forward.

In our book, we give you the blueprint on how to build a successful business from scratch with all the nuts and bolts. It's hard work but attainable if you *really* want it. Our focus is on franchises because most people don't understand that a franchise is a real business. What we mean by *real* is you can't just hit the go button and then fall asleep while others do your work. You must get up and work! The owners are the ones running our operations. You can be an owner-operator too.

As we began building our business, we faced many struggles. Do you want to know why? We were not taught how to build a franchise. Nobody gave us the blueprint on how to do it or held our hands to walk us through the process. All we saw was the finished product. From first-hand experience, we realized there was a lack of information on how to do business. We had watched the people who did it. We saw the finished product, but it was clear nobody had taken the time to document a step-by-step process on how to get it done.

Knowing what we know now, we wish someone would have sat us down and said, "Clint and DeAnna, this is how you build the brand. Here are the steps. Call me with questions, and I will walk you through it." That didn't happen and because of it, we failed at our first shot. Heck, we had a couple of failures! However, we found a way to fail into success. Failing became our first attempt in learning, but thankfully, we continued to learn every step of the way until we started to master what we were called to do.

Now, as a couple, we want to share with you how we built our franchise so you can ride the waves with us and then teach others. This is how we *all* make it. You rarely see couples doing business together or building a franchise; you see individuals. It's rare to see couples in the grind together – unless it's in ministry.

Black couples succeeding together is vital to us because Black business ownership is our ministry. We want to help build a foundation for Black families to be strengthened. Furthermore, we want to set up a legacy, not just for *our* children but for other families' children to have generational wealth. We can do this by teaching others and encouraging each one to teach one.

It took us a while to build multiple franchises and after fifteen years of building, it is time to share the wealth. In this book, we discuss the wealth of understanding, the wealth of knowledge, and the wealth of faith, family, and franchise. You will learn why we couldn't just build the business overnight and how we needed to fail, adjust, rebuild, and double up to get to where we are now.

Timing is everything. That includes the timing of this book. Every piece of this information is critical. It wouldn't have made the book if we had become an overnight success. Read this book, digest it, and plan. We will help you make that plan.

As you read, your mind will open up to business from a husband's (Clint) and wife's (DeAnna) perspective, separately, in our own words. We reveal every single step, move, grind, and hustle, as well as the sweat, tears, growth, and success we experienced that could possibly be shared in a book. You will learn valuable life and business lessons. The ones we hold sacred like staying humble, never boasting, bragging, or showing off; those we learned through trial and error, like never quitting.

We want this book to be interactive, so we wrap up each chapter with a summation of our thoughts and some homework for you. One of the things we found missing in most books, courses, and guides was the actual process of what to do. To remedy this, we created a process section that follows each chapter, so you can begin your journey. You will know exactly what to do by reading the simple steps we give you to move forward. Remember, this is how we became successful. It worked for us, and we believe it can work for you.

Looking back to where we began, we really went through some messes. We didn't know at the time that one step would open multiple doors. And each time we made a move, it would take us onto something bigger and better – even when that bigger and better presented a challenge. The challenges just made us stronger.

It's funny to consider so many who say we made it. You see, when you're on a constant grind, you never look back and say to yourself, "Wow, we made it. Look at this accomplishment." It's hard to see that accomplishment while continuing to grow the business. However, as we reflect on how far we've come, we recognize we have created something noteworthy. Therefore, we are excited to help others jump into the fire as well.

We mean it when we say "fire" too! People look at our success and think our journey was a breeze, but it wasn't, and it still isn't! We've had some heated "fire type" moments. And even now, we don't go to sleep until the stores close at midnight. Once they close, there's usually a two-hour drive home. It works for us, though. During that drive, we discuss our next moves.

One of those moves was putting our journey in a book because we are confident we have a story to tell. God gave us the word to open our franchises; we consulted Him on writing this book too. Whether opening the business or writing a book, we grow stronger as a couple, doing things together and consulting with the Lord. But what makes all of this really work is having a dream to do something and living it out loud.

Living your dreams out loud is the best decision you will ever make. Our dream to be servant leaders means we plan to help each other and you. This book and our businesses are vehicles that bring our dreams to fruition. Now, it's your turn. We want to give you everything possible to succeed with what God promised you. During the process, we thank God for allowing the journey and the lessons.

Are you ready to receive your blessings? Do you want to live your dreams out loud? Good! We are ready to share what God has blessed us with. We pray you will receive everything He has for you. Remember, *you* are the only one with the power to receive what's for you. Stay focused. Take notes. Get ready for the next level!

You can do anything with Faith, Family, and Franchise!

WHO ARE WE?

Lesson 1

CLINT

There was never a moment I can remember where I wasn't an entrepreneur. I went from selling tapioca pudding and Toll House cookies in elementary school, to stocks and insurance sales as a young adult. I sold just about everything. Selling came naturally to me. There is something about the way my brain ticks that makes me want to fulfill the needs of people. I find the gap between what they have and what they need. Then I find a way to monetize it. My leadership skills began early. I was successful in finding the shortest and quickest way to monetization. That was and still is my gift. It works in everything I apply myself to.

I find the gap between what they have and what they need.

This isn't a boisterous type of leadership, though. As a kid, I was kind of quiet – didn't do much talking. But if I saw a gap, I was comfortable speaking up and stepping in to fill it. Growing up in a middle class, South Pasadena family where my mom was a government employee and my dad an engineer, I didn't need much. My parents never stopped me from taking on new sales projects. I saved a lot of money whenever I sold something. Some might say I had it made by high school because I was an athlete too.

Basketball was my sport. When it came to being popular in school, if you were an athlete with some money in your pocket, you could win friends easily. As a young adult, I was one of the first people in my circle to get a car, so that added to my popularity – which, by the way, I never sought – but had by default.

My heart has always been generous. With that, I guess I had even more friends (and so-called friends) around. Giving has always been easy for me because things seem to work out for me. That I attribute to my mindset. I've always known that I could have what I wanted by applying myself. Even if something falls short, I don't get upset. Instead, I aim higher.

A good example was when it came to going to college. My parents were college educated, but they were not stepping up to pay for me to go to college. They had given my older sister and me a good foundation and expected us to figure out college on our own. They didn't help with financial aid applications or anything; so I decided to go to junior college during my first year playing basketball. During that time, I also started my financial consultancy company. The company educated consumers on how to get loans by increasing their creditworthiness. Fortunately, the business was successful, and I sat out my second year of college. Eventually, I returned to a theological seminary and studied for four years only to find out it wasn't an accredited program.

Imagine going to school all that time and not having an accredited degree in the end. For me, it wasn't as devastating because, at eighteen, I was saved and turned my life over to the Lord. Going to theological seminary was my way of having an even closer walk with God. It was an accountability factor in assuring I knew and understood the Word better. It also strengthened my faith and convinced me I could get through and accomplish anything.

With this attitude, I was able to find my way through school, work with different businesses, and launch my own businesses. Having worked in varied ventures and serving multiple roles, I've learned to "roll with the punches." Not too many things shake me or my spirit.

On the personal side, there was a lot going on in my life as well. Business maturity and personal maturity go hand in hand.

Business maturity and personal maturity go hand in hand.

DEANNA

My mother gave birth to me in Bakersfield, California, where she lived with her parents – who would become my guardians because of my mother's substance abuse. I learned a lot from that experience. I saw how substance abuse impacts families. I saw my mom and how she behaved. I heard my grandparents telling her to leave because they couldn't see her like that. I witnessed my mom being abused by men and wheeled into an ambulance after a cruel beating. And I was one of four children split apart. We were separated and placed in the homes of our fathers (yes, there were three different fathers) or in the case of my sister and me, with my grandparents. My brothers stayed with their dads.

This may sound like a tragic beginning in a young person's life, but it was the ultimate blessing to be raised by my grandparents. They were stable and established. By the time I reached middle school, they were retired homeowners. Because of them, I had a solid foundation. As a little girl being raised by older parents who loved and spoiled me, I learned early on what *not* to do. My grandparents raised me in the church where I learned many lessons – good and bad. The best of them was to love the Lord.

During my middle school years, I learned what it was like to be the girl who was last, not having parents to defend or champion for me. And this occurred at church! Shame on them! Nevertheless, it ended up being okay because I learned from some of those parishioners' mean-spirited actions.

I remember wanting to change my last name to my grandparents' last name. I honed in on the "guardian" part of their care for me and wanted people to think they were my parents. Having matching names would be a way for me to achieve this deception. All of that was me trying to find a way to fit in and understand better who I was and how to feel about my situation. However, my grandparents were good, old-fashioned, honest people, so their stance was to be truthful.

To avoid any hurt from others, I became a jokester. When I heard people talking and felt they might be attacking me, I quickly built up a wall of comedy, so I could get them before they got me. Laughing at myself lessened the blow of them laughing at me.

By the time I got to high school, my mom would show up. To null the immense pain I felt, I would say something mean before anyone else could. Funny enough, most of my friends were not mean-spirited. They would give my mom a hug when they saw her. These great friendships and sisterhood molded me. My girlfriends supported me and didn't judge.

As I grew older, popularity continued to be my main interest rather than schoolwork; I was an average student because of this. Yet, I wasn't a wild, crazy, party person even though I would party. There was no way I was going to do what my mom, aunts, and uncles did with their lives. I never understood how they were so out there when they had such "chill" parents. My parents, aunts, and uncles were off the chain but my grandparents were totally different! I'll never know that story.

After growing up and graduating high school, I got accepted to California State Dominguez Hills College. I left Bakersfield so that I could see the world. It wasn't long before I realized how easy it was to screw up, even having solid grandparents in my corner.

Being accepted into college is totally different from being prepared for it.

Being accepted into college is totally different from being prepared for it. I wasn't prepared. My grandparents were older, and their focus was more on me finding work after high school. From their generational knowledge, if you finish high school and get a good government job with benefits, you've made it. They didn't know how to help me navigate college. In that space, I was on my own – even though they supported me financially.

When my grades lagged, I decided to withdraw and go to El Camino, a junior college. How backward was that? Well, I knew I didn't want to return to Bakersfield, so this was my solution, along with finding a job.

CLINT AND DEANNA

We were basically two kids from California: Pasadena and Bakersfield. We didn't know each other growing up, but we both knew the Lord. That connection had to be intact for us to end up together. The onset was our affiliation with a young adult group at the Peace Apostolic Church in Carson. At the time, the church was in Inglewood. There were probably 400 to 500 people at the church with a sub-stantial youth population between eighteen and twenty-five.

As part of this young adult population, we wanted to know and learn more about the Word, so it made sense to hang out with like-minded people. Our group wasn't into clubs, drinking, hustling, or being on the streets. Our peer pressure was to live for God as best we could. In this group of about thirty people, we were encouraged to stay committed to the Lord. We became friends and a lot of people were hooking up and becoming couples too. Clint's first wife was in the group, and we all knew each other. Many of the couples who got together in that group are still married today and so are our friends. We can all go back to the same roots. Between Clint and me, we go back twenty-eight to thirty years consistently at that church.

We were great friends and that was probably the best way for us to end up together. Before connecting with each other in a romantic way, we were in other relationships that hurt us deeply. Hence, we were both vulnerable but also stronger. We had no interest whatsoever in tolerating any crap. We decided to make a deliberate, strong commitment to each other. Neither of us wanted to be hurt again, so this was something we needed to be sure about. After twenty-two years, I guess you can say we were pretty sure, but it had to be right. We needed it to be in divine order.

SCRIPTURES

For the love of money is a root of all kinds of evil. Some people, eager for money, have wandered from the faith and pierced themselves with many griefs.
(1 Timothy 6:10 NIV)

In everything I did, I showed you that by this kind of hard work we must help the weak, remembering the words the Lord Jesus himself said: 'It is more blessed to give than to receive.' (Acts 20:35 NIV)

But if serving the LORD seems undesirable to you, then choose for yourselves this day whom you will serve, whether the gods your ancestors served beyond the Euphrates, or the gods of the Amorites, in whose land you are living. But as for me and my household, we will serve the LORD. (Joshua 24:15 NIV)

7

PROCESS

What you just read in Lesson 1 was all about us: Clint and DeAnna. Now, we want you to take this chapter and make it about you. This book is for couples, so we hope you and your significant other are reading it together. If not, there are some questions for you too. Answer the following questions to be in touch with who you are and who is in your corner. Once you answer questions like these, you will be able to better understand where and how you fit into the business world.

1. Who are you? Where and how did you grow up? How did that impact who you are today?
2. What do you want? How do you plan to get it?
3. Who is in your corner? Are you married? Does your spouse also want to have a business? If not, how will you communicate your dreams?
4. How do you and your significant other/partner communicate? Can you improve on it? How?

After you've addressed these questions, sit down with your significant other or partner and go over the answers you both shared. This is one of the first steps in communicating effectively.

IN DIVINE ORDER

Lesson 2

DEANNA

Clint was very handsome and tall – which was no secret. I liked him. He carried himself in a very masculine, confident way. Actually, he seemed too young to be so sure of himself. At only twenty years old, he knew where he was going and could hold intriguing conversations. He was also very curt. Most folks still say Clint is a little tough, but he was always cool and friendly to me. He was a little lighter in complexion than the guys I typically dated, but he was cute! We clicked and had an attraction as friends when we first met. Clint would talk to me about pretty much anything. We never hooked up romantically. We were just friends but the truth is I always felt a strong attraction to him. The chemistry was there.

While I attended the church, I dated a guy for about three years, and we got engaged. He was in the music industry, had three kids, was divorced, and about nine years older than I was. Being with him meant I would be taking on a lot. The truth of the matter is I probably wanted a marriage more than he was ready to commit to a marriage. We got engaged, but I don't think he ever

9

had any intentions of marrying me. Nevertheless, I was planning for a wedding. Literally, I set a date, had the bridesmaids fitted for dresses, did cake samplings, and even met with the First Lady for colors and decorations. I was in full swing, but he wasn't. He seemed pressured by his family that I wasn't the ideal "church lady" for him. He kept delaying the wedding until, eventually, we called it off. That breakup was devastating and filled with embarrassment for me. Think about an entire church hearing about a wedding that never came to fruition. It was awful!

I went back to school and prepared myself for an aggressive campaign to be better.

I went back to school and prepared myself for an aggressive campaign to be better at work and to succeed. My emotional state was such that I didn't want to lose anymore. Coming out of that bad relationship and facing my family and friends to let them know I wasn't getting married was tough.

As time went on, the strong feelings I had for Clint resurfaced. I liked him very much, but I guarded my heart because I didn't want to be hurt again. I got on the grind and made my money from working hard. Making more money meant I could shop, change cars when I wanted, and pile up debt. Yes, I was in a broken state when I reconnected with Clint. It just so happened he was in a broken state too because he was divorced from his wife. We were getting by, but we had both been through the fire.

CLINT

Back when we originally met, everyone was hooking up, but I had my eyes elsewhere before getting with Deanna. As friends, Deanna and I were always cool. When we first met, I didn't know her age, but she was obviously a couple of years older because she was working for the county and had her own place. She was and still is attractive to me. I'd tease her about her figure and her lips. I mean, Deanna was stacked! Again, we were just friends. I ended up marrying someone else who was a part of our group.

I loved being married then – just like I love being married now. And, my first marriage wasn't a bad one. I think I just didn't really know how to be married at the time. As a young man, I was not as mindful as I could have been. That was a mistake. I thought marriage was about working hard, going home every night to my wife, and taking a trip every now and then. I didn't realize that

Creating a network of people to love and support you is essential to growth.

wasn't enough. My first wife wanted things to be different. I didn't know how to fulfill her needs. She was only nineteen, going to school, and still figuring out her career, while I was already into my career, buying my first house at twenty, and making six figures. I had to work long, hard hours for that, so I got her a dog as a companion instead of me. I didn't realize until it was too late that the dog wouldn't be enough. She left me in the middle of the night.

It was devastating. I went through quite a time trying to save the marriage, but it wasn't happening. She served me papers at work within less than sixty days of walking out the door. I was very hurt, but she had no aspirations to reconcile with me at all. After receiving the papers, I pretty much stopped trying and delved into work. My work excelled, and I started buying cars and clothes as an outlet to soothe my pain. Those were some of my best business years because I was on the grind and 100 percent focused on work.

At that point and time, I just wasn't ready to settle down again. I'd already been married at a young age, so now I just wanted companionship: going out to eat, listening to jazz, and other activities you want to share with someone. That's all I wanted to do. So I dated people. Deanna was someone I could always talk to. She would give consultation and prayer, not really advice. She gave me the space to talk.

DEANNA AND CLINT

Not even a kiss! Yes, believe it! It's possible. (Sigh.)

We started talking on the phone, at times, even falling asleep on the other end when Clint was going through his divorce. It was an emotional experience for him. Some days, he was nice but on other days, he was a little short! While going through the divorce, his ex-wife entered the courtroom pregnant with someone else's child. That hurt!

Clint's divorce was final at the end of July 1995. Both of our relationships were over and we went out on our first date after his divorce. I asked Clint, why now? He said, "I'm celebrating my divorce." The next thing you know, we were courting. It was obvious we were attracted to each other. However, people would say Clint wasn't interested in settling down after dealing with the emotions of the divorce. They were correct! He was hurt and scared.

Our courtship began when we were both vulnerable but we always enjoyed each other's company. We found it easy to talk to each other. But admittedly, we weren't just talking. We may have put a little too much confidence in our flesh. In July of 1997, we found out we were pregnant with our first child – Clinton Jr. (CJ). This was totally frowned upon in our church community and frankly, even by us. However, we had to decide if we were going to

Long Beach, CA. Christmas 2015

church for the people or for the love of Christ. As much as we loved the church, we were not always encouraged by the people during moments of adversity.

This was an embarrassing time. It was tough. However, it was a part of our journey. Hence, we took responsibility and began to walk.

This may come as a surprise to Deanna, but by this time, I knew I wanted to settle down and have a family. Honestly, I knew when CJ was conceived. It wasn't necessarily planned, but I was sure if it were the case, I'd be happy about it.

Deanna picked me up from the airport when I returned from a funeral in New Orleans. On the way home, she told me she was pregnant. She was nervous but ready to be a mom. I was eager to take on the responsibility of a dad.

Despite not being married first, we believe God was long-suffering with us. Indeed, He is rich in grace and mercy. At seven months pregnant, we

CJ's high school graduation from St. John Bosco HS Bellflower, CA. May 2016

decided to get married. Then we faced the situation together. This was a very challenging test of our commitment to each other, but we pushed through. We stood hand in hand in front of everybody – knowing the whispers and talk were all about us.

At the end of the day, it was (and still is) God and us. God has the final say. We were married by Pastor Howard A. Swancy, Jr. on December 5, 1997, and CJ was born on February 12, 1998.

Our union and the blessing of our son brought us closer to the Lord and to each other. We had to be committed. That meant finding ways to ensure we stayed close to God and His Word. Establishing close relationships with our pastor and setting ourselves up for spiritual mentoring were two ways we found to keep that commitment.

The next year, March 3, 1999, our precious baby girl, Cydni, was born – no turning back, we were all in. We were determined to work for our family.

Cydni's graduation from Mater Dei High School
at UC Irvine. May 2017

Sisterhood, 40 years strong: Tonya Bealey, Regina Shelton,
Mechelle Henry, Philashone Myers, Lady Vicki Kemp,
DeAnna, Marika Walker, Stacey Williams. April 2018

The Husbands, Brothers for Life – Group Date Night at Fogo De Chao
in Beverly Hills: Clint, Bishop Vernon Kemp, Jimmy Henry, Brandon
Shelton, Walter Williams, Dennis Schaffer. March 2018

Mentoring for us included learning how to sustain a successful marriage and raise a godly family in a worldly environment. Developing relationships like these helped us stay the course. These mentors are part of a network of blessings that we've established and grown.

On receiving these blessings, we realize our lives were created by divine order. The path we walked from childhood was designed just for us. Whether being raised by grandparents or having to pay for our own education,

The Fav Couples – Clint and DeAnna, Vernon and Vicki Kemp, Brandon and Regina Shelton, Daniel and Geneva Jordan, in Cabo San Lucas. September 2019

each step, obstacle, and challenge brought us where we are today.

Staying in divine order means staying the course with God. Growing with the Lord is not always easy, especially when working as a family unit where we all have our own ideas and goals. Mentors and guides are very important.

Now, over twenty years after taking our vows and staying the course, we still have mentors and ask for guidance. There is no perfect path but creating a network of people to love and support you along the way is essential to growth. The network of supporters included our pastor but there

20th wedding anniversary vacation at the Royal Caribbean Resort in Ocho Rios Jamaica. January 2018

were other everyday people like us.

Finding like-minded people is the key to building faith, family, and franchise. Our like-mindedness had to do with surrounding ourselves with God-fearing people who wanted to grow in the ways of the Lord.

Pastor Howard A. Swancy Jr. – Annual Peace Apostolic Church Family Vacation Baha Mar Resort, Nassau Bahamas. July 2019

Whether in our personal lives or in business, we always looked for people who had a spiritual basis. In the process of this progressive growth, we too, have become mentors.

Mentoring and guiding those who are like-minded is part of our calling that we do every day. It worked for us over the years, and we want to give back what we've benefitted from. We are open to working with anyone who wants to build a business or sustain a strong family. The premise is to understand we do it through a walk with God. That keeps us on the divinely ordered path.

Greater Harvest Marriage Retreat in Ventura, CA. November 2018

Dr. Angel Schaffer – Trip to Havana Cuba
(aka Thelma and Louise LOL). January 2019

SCRIPTURES

Plans fail for lack of counsel, but with many advisers they succeed. (Proverbs 15:22 NIV)

Where no counsel is, the people fall: but in the multitude of counsellors there is safety. (Proverbs 11:14)

If any of you lacks wisdom, you should ask God, who gives generously to all without finding fault, and it will be given to you. (James 1:5 NIV)

PROCESS

Having a guide or mentor can be the difference between making good or bad decisions at critical moments in your life. Yes, instinct and prayer are always good guides; however, seeking counsel from an expert or godly people can give you the confirmation you need as you journey along your path.

1. Write down one or two counselors whom you can call on for relationship advice. If you can't think of any, start searching for those who help keep you in touch with the love you began your coupledom in.
2. Think about mentors/guides who can offer sound advice as you consider entering a business venture. You're not looking for a "yes" person but someone who will speak the truth and light into your situation.

When you've identified these mentors/guides, make sure they know you are counting on them to be there for you. Finally, appreciate them, not just with words of thanks. Send a card or token of appreciation every now and then letting them know their counsel is beneficial.

ENTREPRENEURSHIP VERSUS A JOB

Lesson 3

DEANNA

Growing up, I loved watching the news and had always dreamed of being a television anchor. I didn't dream of being a doctor or lawyer like many young people do; that wasn't tied to my personality. No, I was an extrovert, a talker. I liked talking. In my mind, being an anchor would allow me to connect with an audience in a big way every night on television. Funny how your dreams stick with you as you grow into adulthood. The anchor desires faded away, but I still enjoy talking to people.

In my family, we were taught that getting a good government job was about as secure and successful as you could get. After all, my grandparents retired from secure positions, and they lived comfortably. With this mindset, I went after a job with the county.

I worked with LA County in November of 1990. My cousin, Shawn, was a student worker and told me about a clerical position that opened there. I'd already worked with temporary agencies in retail and at a bank, so I had mastered some clerical skills. The position was for an eligibility worker. The process to get the job was parallel to how people view the county overall. It was a bit insensitive and sterile.

First, the room was full of people who signed up to take the placement test. We all tested together, and afterward, we sat in the testing room, waiting. No instructions were given about what would happen next. We just sat and waited. Eventually, someone came and divided us into groups, not telling us whether we were in a group that passed or failed the test. Again, we sat and waited until we were called to speak with someone. Obviously, I must have been in the group that passed the test because I was offered a position and asked which office I wanted to work from.

Why I chose the Imperial and Normandie office is beyond me. Honestly, I had no idea which office to choose or what I was getting myself into. On the map, it was the closest location to my apartment in Hawthorne. This was the beginning of my career as a Los Angeles County worker. I was venturing into the unknown. That was just the beginning of the shocking experience I was in for.

Reporting for my first day of work at the Imperial and Normandie office was crazy. The location landed me at a warehouse-type place where I entered through the back door and saw a room full of desks. After working with temporary agencies and being in banks, I was used to functioning in professional environments and wearing professional clothes. This place was the opposite of that. I was escorted to "administration" in the middle of nowhere. No one told me anything. They literally gave me a chair to sit in where I stayed for four hours with no one saying one word to me.

Finally, the same secretary who instructed me to sit in that space came out and said, "Oh, you're still here? You can go to lunch." That was it. Sit. Go to lunch. This was so confusing to me. I called my grandmother to tell her what happened. I explained that no one was speaking to me. I thought they were talking *about* me rather than *with* me. My grandmother told me to just follow the instructions and go back to work. After lunch, I returned, and they sent me to probably one of the sweetest people I'd ever met. I was introduced to Mrs. Ross who introduced me to LA County. That introduction included teaching me patience, how to get along with people, and the most valuable lesson of all – how to be thick-skinned.

Learning what my duties included meant understanding how to work with people. On top of it all, I got my childhood dream – sort of. I was talking to people all the time! My caseload was 80% African-American men between the ages of eighteen to sixty. I had to work with them on lots of issues. However, they weren't the ones causing all the drama at work. Nope! That was sufficiently handled by my co-workers. I witnessed co-workers fighting, being arrested, and doing just about any inappropriate thing you can think of while working at Imperial and Normandie.

No matter how much drama I experienced in that job, I took it as a lesson. Those experiences taught me how to work with people in all sorts of situations. Having all that drama at work made my home a refuge. I lived with a roommate up until I got married – drama-free. Lessons from the field! That being said, knowing what was required of the job was great, even if the environment was less than desired. These life lessons informed me of the path I wanted to chart. My goal was to be a human resources director.

People in my circle were proud and that also inspired me.

I wasn't the only one with goals for me. Sure enough, my grandparents envisioned me in this job for life. When I got the job, my grandmother was so excited. She announced at church that I got a "good county job." She was more excited about that than about my getting into college! I had hit the jackpot and was set for life as far as they were concerned. You see, that's the way their generation made it. Learning from them, I felt like I'd made it too. People in my circle were proud and that also inspired me.

The job was stable and secure. That was good but working for the county was not for the faint at heart. The bickering, bad attitudes, and straight-up fights were like going into a war zone every day. I liked having a job, but I didn't want to stay in that environment. When I saw my coworkers transferring, moving on, and getting promoted, I got a new motivation. It wasn't enough to just have a good county job. I wanted to grow and build a career too.

With this motivation to move up in management, I decided to return to school to get my degree. My roommate Angelia and friend Ingrid encouraged me to continue my educational journey. We all knew any upward movement would rely on having that paper in hand; it was all about promotion.

While pregnant with my son, I went back to school. By the time I was pregnant with my daughter, I had passed the exam for the supervisor position. After nine years of working with the county, I was ready to move up. The problem was an opportunity came up while I was out on maternity leave; these positions didn't come around often. The only way to get the job was to return to work. I'd just delivered my daughter but after speaking with Clint and my doctor, I was back on the job.

CJ's Freshman Intake weekend at Morehouse College in Atlanta. August 2016

I signed my papers to become a supervisor. My career advancement with the county was underway.

A couple of things that I really appreciated about having a county job were the benefits and the consistent pay. On the fifteenth and the thirtieth, I could count on having money. I also had good insurance with a low copay to support the family. Having two brand new babies, I needed good insurance and a steady income. Especially when finding out my daughter had asthma.

Cydni's college signing day at Mater Dei HS Santa Ana, CA. Fall 2016

Not that Clint wasn't working. He always had a project underway. Clint was the entrepreneur and optimist, while I felt the need to have a "stable job." I was of the mindset that entrepreneurship was good, but we needed something definite because we had babies.

At the county, I got promoted to different departments because of my good work ethics. As I moved up the career ladder, I landed positions I enjoyed. The last position I had was with the elderly and disabled, ensuring they received the care they needed to remain in their homes. That was probably one of the best positions I had with the county. It gave me more compassion. It was incomprehensible how people left their parents to figure things out on their own as they aged. In my family, no matter what the dysfunction, we were going to figure it out together. Doing well was important to me, and this position allowed me to do just that, help an underserved population.

While I was doing well at the county and Clint's businesses were taking off, I returned to school for my master's degree. My high school counselor in Bakersfield was my inspiration. She had always told me about the importance of college, and we were closely connected. I wanted to look out for other young Black girls the way she had looked out for me. Remembering this connection, my new mission was to become a school counselor for middle or high school girls.

This goal became so real to me that I began applying for jobs at schools. Unfortunately, without classroom experience, I wasn't getting any traction. It was discouraging. Eventually, I gave up. Between 2002 and 2006, Clint was bringing in good money and my county job was paying off too. We were investing in properties and wanted to do something more. This was between 2002 and 2006. Clint and I decided to look at franchises.

We landed a Wingstop franchise. Then came the hardest decision I ever had to make: leaving LA County. That might sound ridiculous to you, but the county had done me well. Also, I had been brainwashed to believe you don't walk away from a "good county job." The county job meant stability. I already knew what it felt like when Clint did his own thing. At the beginning of those business ventures, we raised a family on one income, and it worked. However, even with that, my mind was made up that no matter what, I wouldn't leave my county job.

We opened the Wingstop. It started out as an average store, but there was a lot to be done to run a business like that. I trained in Dallas, Texas, for three full weeks learning the Wingstop way. You could say it was like going to a Wingstop Academy. I got all the training and brought it back to train others. Clint took some of the nuggets I gave and taught himself the Wingstop way. I resigned from the county and managed our restaurant business full time, while Clint ran his many other businesses. Clint and I were really restaurateurs now.

I trained in Dallas, Texas, for three full weeks learning the Wingstop way.

CLINT

I never had a job that consisted of guaranteed pay. Even when working for someone else, I worked on commission. Besides being an entrepreneur since childhood, I guess you could say my first professional job was in debt collection; that lasted about four years. It was dialing for dollars. I literally had to call people for collections when they bounced checks, were late on medical bills, or for payments on leased cars. This was not easy work. I saw guys eating Ramen noodles for lunch and I saw guys doing well. I wanted to do well, so I steadily crept up the sales board.

At the same time I was doing debt collection, I created Consumer Advisor Service Experts to advise people on how to better navigate credit and financial systems. I always had a business. Maybe I was born an entrepreneur because it just comes naturally for me to run things and operate companies.

In everything I did, I would ask God for help, knowing He could pull me through. When the numbers were low or if something wasn't going as I thought it should, I'd just ask Him, "What are You going to do? You've never forsaken me." And as always, He came through. Outside of two times when I was down, I never had a bad month. I've made over six figures since I was twenty years old.

God is truly a miracle worker but don't get confused about how He works. He requires us to do some work too. It's not just saying a prayer and having things appear. God expects you to work both spiritually and physically. At work, I was the first in and the last out most of the time. If the job required 100 calls, I'd make 150 or 200. Whether I had to meet people in person or get them on the phone, I did what it took to be successful. I'm a natural introvert, but the work I did demanded I be an extrovert. So wherever people gathered, I would put myself in those places to speak. As far as my spirituality is concerned, once I got saved, I longed for a closer walk with Christ.

As I said before, this desire was so strong, I even went to theology school for a better connection.

No matter what it took to succeed, I was determined to walk that walk. When I worked in the insurance industry and needed to bring others into the business, I sought out professionals to recruit into the agency. I also looked for couples with kids because I could relate to them with a shared experience. Sales and respect for the customer are vital in the insurance business. Without them, you can lose your advanced commissions if the person doesn't maintain the insurance policy. Something like this will have you in a hole at the start of the month. That was not an option for me. So every day, I would find people who wanted to use our services.

My business sales motto was "5 to survive and 10 to win." That meant I needed to move past survival mode and into a thriving mentality. With that philosophy, I could get two sales instead of one.

I was good at sales and made a living in the cold market until it became warm. I worked the marketplace with pride. At times, I would share my story of being a new husband and father to break into a conversation or ask people to share their contacts to help me stay employed. There was no shame in doing my job. I did it well. When people said no to an

All my professional life, I've competed with myself to bring out the best in me.

opportunity with me, it was okay because I knew each "no" was leading me to my "yes." I was also good at collections using innovative tactics. Sometimes I'd offer people deals like waiving the interest and reducing the principal. This would get my numbers up by the end of the month. At the end of the day, debtors would send me cards thanking me for working with them. All my professional life, I've competed with myself to bring out the best in me. In the process, I've mastered bringing out the best in others.

Before getting married, I always earned my money from business. I did well. When I was out with friends, it was standard that if I ate, everyone ate – on me. But with two babies in diapers and a wife, making five to ten thousand dollars a month wasn't going to be enough to keep up that type of lifestyle. I had to think bigger because I wanted to provide for my family and ensure they had everything they needed.

In September 1999, I left Primerica Financial Services with a fellow regional vice president, Tracy Felton, and started Felton and Lewis Financial Group.

In 2001, we were in partnership with an insurance agency. We were doing well. Unfortunately, our business partner lost his son in the 9/11 Towers attack and left the company. This turn of events made Deanna and me look at things differently. We were doing well between the two of us and had made significant strides. Still, with the sudden loss of my partner, the compass changed. I began to focus more on the real estate side of my business. This focus was well centered. The business took off as if the market were just waiting for me to enter.

Between 2002 and 2004, we were making tens of thousands of dollars a month. Deanna had her steady county position, and my real estate loans, as well as property sales, brought in up to two-and-a-half million dollars in commissions. I'm licensed in both real estate and lending, so I could walk away from a purchase with property and money.

We invested in property and owned three in Arizona, three in Southern CA, two in Bakersfield, and one condo in Lake Tahoe. We were in a groove and began to think we wanted our money to work even harder for us.

DeAnna and I brainstormed on ideas all the time. At this point, we talked about other business opportunities like franchises. We liked to eat out and recognized that in Bakersfield where DeAnna was born and raised, there weren't a lot of restaurant choices. That's where the restaurant idea came from. We researched owning a restaurant: McDonald's, Burger King, Quiznos. Basically, we needed to figure out what the best one was for our area.

DeAnna and I brainstormed on ideas all the time.

Deanna had done research since her social worker days, so she was all over it. I positioned us to be credit-ready for an opportunity. We had good credit and money in the bank because of cash flow. But we needed other things in place to purchase a franchise – that's what I was good at.

I positioned our financials (i.e., tax returns) to be ready for a franchise. Writing things off on taxes doesn't always look good to lenders. They don't want to see negative income. They need to see earnings. On paper, we needed to look worthy enough to purchase a business. During 2004 and 2005, we focused on getting those things in order.

Once the paperwork was in order, our credit looked great. We were what I call financially fit and ready. We were prepared to introduce ourselves to our franchise of choice – Wingstop. We went to Texas to meet our representatives. They knew exactly what we knew – that Bakersfield Wingstop was ours.

Asking DeAnna to quit her job and help with the business was one of the hardest things I had to do. I was used to making things happen on my own and letting her remain in her groove. But business was good, and I needed her. We needed to do this venture together. Once we discussed it, we were in it to win it – together.

DEANNA AND CLINT

We had no idea that being restaurateurs would be in our future when we first got married. Hey, having one person working a steady job and the other running a successful business could have been enough. We could have made our money and gone for the cars, jet skis, and other comforts or frivolous stuff. That would have been just fine. But that wasn't enough for God, so it wasn't enough for us. We know, by no uncertain terms, that Wingstop was a God thing.

You see, we were doing pretty darn good when we started our search into franchises. Our discussions were around finding a business that was community-driven but once we began looking at franchises, we never turned back. The research extended to every type of franchise you could think of. Somehow, we landed in the food arena with our top three being Wingstop, Subway, and Jamba Juice.

When we say we did the research – trust us – we did the research. Remember, DeAnna had acquired investigative research skills from working with the county, and I had entrepreneurial skills. Researching this industry was critical for our success. We know only one ingredient is missing from lots of new business start-ups. Without gathering as much information as possible on a business, you can really have a bad experience down the road.

We put in the research, blood, sweat, and tears to run the business. Still holding both our jobs with the county and in real estate, we started pulling things together and doing our homework. By the time we decided on Wingstop, we were prepared to go to them and make an offer – and we did. We flew to Texas to meet with one of their salespeople, Bruce.

We put in the research, blood, sweat, and tears to run the business.

Bruce took us around and showed us the landscape of the business. He discussed what was already in existence and what was coming. The map he showed us had thumbtacks all over it, and it also confirmed the research we had done for ourselves. There were wide-open territories for Wingstop and Bakersfield was one of them. Throughout the entire time, we had prepared ourselves for the franchise, we also checked out locations and knew Bakersfield was our market.

Now to back it up a bit, Wingstop was on our list because whenever we had a party or gathering at the house, we would order Wingstop. One day while ordering, we realized how simple the menu was. We thought if they were a franchise, it would fit right up our alley. Checking into it, we discovered, in fact, they were a franchise. So we continued our research from there. Finding something we liked or found value in was part of the research. You'll learn more about finding your niche later.

The desire, research, preparation of the finances, and agreement to work together were all the beginning of our franchise ownership. It sounds like four easy steps, but each was an individual campaign of discussion, contemplation, and making a final decision together. And working together as a couple was at the core of each step. Without an agreement, even the idea couldn't come to fruition. We had to be in alignment with each other step-by-step.

At times, we were not in sync. Clint is the business guy so when there was fear about moving forward, I had no fear in saying, "Break it down, Babe," and he would. One thing is for sure: dealing with finances can break a couple down. It can literally destroy a marriage. If you research the top three reasons for divorce, you will find money right behind infidelity. It's probably why people misquote Scripture saying *money* is the root of all evil when it actually says, "The *love of* money is the root of all evil" (1 Timothy 6:10). Money can make or break you. However, that didn't happen to us. For some reason, the financial struggles brought us closer together. And that theory would be tested time and time again, especially in owning a franchise.

SCRIPTURES

All the believers were together and had everything in common. They sold property and possessions to give to anyone who had need. (Acts 2:44-45 NIV)

Two are better than one, because they have a good return for their labor: If either of them falls down, one can help the other up. But pity anyone who falls and has no one to help them up. (Ecclesiastes 4:9-10 NIV)

Even so faith, if it hath not works, is dead, being alone. (James 2:17)

PROCESS

Couples must bring balance to their lives together and still appreciate individual gifts as well. How well do you master being separate but equal together?

1. Draw a line down the middle of your paper. On the left, write two to three of your partner's unique qualities. On the right side, write your unique qualities or abilities.
2. Discuss what you appreciate about each other's uniqueness. Did your partner write the same thing about him or herself? Did he or she write the same thing you wrote about you?

Having open communication with your partner is the key to starting a business/franchise together.

FINANCIAL AFFAIRS AIN'T EASY

Lesson 4

CLINT

The downturn of our finances happened when the bubble burst right about 2008. We were able to keep the house and one of the businesses but pretty much everything else had to go. For four years, we were painting or packing. We were either in the house fixing it up or packing it up to go.

We were headed toward bankruptcy in the process of letting things go. It not only impacted our belongings but also our credit. Everything went down when the market crashed. We got rid of cars and other depreciating assets. I put a lot of wear and tear on vehicles going back and forth, so we used rentals. When you rent a car, you don't have to claim it as property. With all the mileage I was putting on the vehicles, we couldn't qualify to own a car anyway.

Even though the downturn of the market was awful for us, timing was still everything. It didn't

I kept my entrepreneurial spirit with a business of my own.

seem as if I had the time to do anything but, in fact, everything was strategic. My timing wasn't just about the business; it was about family and what was best for them. I would never miss a whole day without seeing the kids. That meant I would drop them off at school and then take the drive to Bakersfield afterward.

I'd work night and day doing two-and-a-half shifts at a time, sometimes sleeping at hotels. But my family would see me in the morning, the night before, and dinner the day after. Technically, I would never miss a day with my family. And on the weekends, we would load up the car with movies and drive. Of course, we would go to work in the store (everyone would work). We would visit family members, often staying overnight, only to come back home and start over every Sunday. This strategy was tough and required many sacrifices, but it worked for us.

Even with the downturn of the market, owning the franchise, and fighting to keep it alive, I kept my entrepreneurial spirit with a business of my own. Some might call it a "side hustle," but it's lasted through time as a sustainable business endeavor.

Generational Wealth, Inc. is a financial advisement firm that teaches people the principles of wealth. I'd done many iterations of this business since high school. Whether through selling insurance or assisting people to restore their credit, it was all leading to Generational Wealth. It helped to keep us afloat during our time of crisis. I still operate this business alongside the franchises today.

How did we manage all of this? In any type of financial endeavor, you must know when to do certain things. At all times, I consulted good counsel and within a year, we were able to rebuild our credit, get a car, and even open a second store. We had earned a lot so when the market turned down, we lost a lot. The key was to be willing to walk away from some of the investments we made. We also had to stick it out together as a couple. DeAnna was the perfect partner because she walked the walk with me – even through the fiercest storm. As a couple in business, you must do that faith walk together or everything will fall apart.

DEANNA

Finally, after Wingstop was opened and Clint couldn't continue doing it on his own, I left my county job. Things were going pretty well. Then, the market crashed in 2008, and with that crash, the business spiraled right down with it. It almost wiped us out.

Folks were not eating out like they had been and business took a dive. We went from making thousands per month to nothing. Even Clint's other businesses were not secure. He went from closing loans to no loans going through. To add insult to injury, I had left my secure job with the county and felt vulnerable.

Clint was doing everything he could to keep us above water, and it was literally making him physically sick. One day, we were sitting on the edge of the bed talking. He said he needed to lie down because he felt lightheaded. I was terrified. Remember, I'm a pessimist, so I instantly thought "heart attack" because he was so stressed.

We were the perfect example of "robbing Peter to pay Paul." It was obvious we were stressed. Seeing Clint like this was crushing me. There was no way I was going to let my husband keep up this hectic pace to get us back on our feet. I made up my mind that the stress and situation were not going to take my husband out. I was going to return to work.

I don't even know if I told Clint I called human resources at the county. I called them to find out about getting reinstated. They told me I had two years to reinstate. I could go back to any position I ever held at the county. That was my answer. God answered every thought and prayer. However, I had to make the calls and get someone to say I could come back. Then they would have to do the paperwork to bring me back. Of course, I had to chuckle at that because no one liked to do paperwork at the county. Still, I knew what I needed to do and got busy.

I had built some bridges there and had kept them all intact.

Fortunately, I had built some bridges throughout my time there and had kept them all intact. I got on a call with one of my girlfriends letting her know what needed to be done. Coincidentally, she just happened to be at a management conference with many of my former department folks. She called me back saying one of my former colleagues, James, had four positions available; one was mine if I wanted. This was a "glory hallelujah" moment.

Just as God would have it, I got reinstated one day shy of my expiration date. Hey, that has me changing the phrase, "He may not come when you want Him, but He's right on time" to "He comes when you want Him and steps in right on time!"

Once rehired, James introduced me to everyone letting them know they might not know me now but I was good. I would be sure to prove him right after he gave me that opportunity. Unfortunately, just a year later, James was playing baseball and ended up having a heart attack. God placed him there for me when I needed it and then he was gone. I was devastated by his death, as was Clint – knowing he was our angel during a crisis. I honored James' word, dusted off my suits, and went back to work.

We still owned the franchise but most people didn't know because it wasn't something I bragged about. I went to work for the county, and I worked!

By 2009, the economy was swinging back up, and our Wingstop boomed again. We couldn't believe it. It was doing so bad that we had it up for sale. Suddenly, it turned, and we agreed if we could maintain it without taking from the household, we'd ride it out. We weren't taking a salary from the store, but we did enough to keep the doors open so we stayed steady.

Of course, as the Wingstop business took an upswing, it was time for me to come back full time. I wanted to keep my foot in the door with the county this time because I had just gotten in by the skin of my *chinny chin chin!*

Still, Clint and I were in business together. Our finances were intertwined just like we were as a family unit. I took a leave of absence (that was my security blanket). Clint and I continued our trek to making the franchise work.

I finally resigned in July 2013, with two stores under our belt because Clint needed me all in. We were secure enough and our finances were intact, but I was afraid of walking away from that check coming in on the fifteenth and the thirtieth, as well as having insurance for my family.

The mentality of being dependent on a government check was real for me, but I also believed in my husband. We were ready.

God always shows you when you believe and are willing to leap.

It was a leap of faith. God always shows you when you believe and are willing to leap. He will catch you. Not only did our businesses prosper, but I found out I still had retirement money with the county I could collect at age fifty. It took me a while to grasp the blessings we had received.

Entrepreneurship is great, but at the end of the day, I have nothing negative to say about LA County. I learned a lot, and it sustained us through some tough times. If I had to dust off my suits and apply again, I would. I've got my degrees. I've got my connections, and I've got my work ethic. I can work. I respect people, and they respect me. It's important how you maintain and leave a job.

It's also important to understand that finances shouldn't make or break your family. Clint and I were in it for the long haul. When we ended up in bankruptcy court, I knew our faith would be tested. Clint understood business and knew what was in store but the bankruptcy court was a shell shocker for me. It felt as if I were in criminal court. Clint didn't tell me much because he knows I get antsy and a bit off-kilter with these types of things. This was where the rubber hit the road and our faith walk really began!

DEANNA AND CLINT

When the business reached the point where it was doing badly, and we were losing our property, we had to go to the bankruptcy court. It's one thing to be able to walk away from things but going bankrupt was a whole different story. This is where our faith really got stronger.

In bankruptcy court, the judge asks questions that can be intimidating – even if you do know what's going on. At some point, the questioning can make you feel you'll be incarcerated. In our case, the judge asked DeAnna questions and wouldn't allow me to help. We wanted to tell him we weren't bad people. We simply invested in a business that wasn't doing so great. In spite of the intimidation and humiliation, we understood the judge was just doing his job and didn't care about our personal story.

Later, we realized as they tallied the list of what we could keep and what we had to get rid of that it was just stuff we could get again. That was the real lesson of the bankruptcy court. We could recover. We still had our health. We still had a family. We still had our experiences and work ethics, and we could start over. We didn't have to stay in a bad position. It was about letting go and letting God do His work to move us forward.

Thank God our kids never were into *stuff*. We had Christmas, birthday gifts, and a big village of people who loved us and would bring us things. It was challenging, but we still had the ability to make money. And once we figured out what we needed, we would put the feelers out and make it happen. Being broke means there's not enough to take care of your liabilities, but it doesn't stop you from moving forward. The bankruptcy released us, so we could do just that.

Here's the interesting thing we saw in bankruptcy court. We were the only Black folks there! You see, they don't tell us about starting over with a clean slate. Many of the people there were saying it wasn't their first time. They'd started over before! What a concept! To release the past and start fresh with a clean slate is freeing.

As African-Americans, we have so much pride when it comes to failing. We don't allow ourselves to fall or fail without being very critical and judgmental. Thinking of bankruptcy puts us in a panic as a people. For us, it says we couldn't cut the mustard or didn't have what it takes.

When you've done your best, there is a way to move forward.

But that's not true. It just means you tried something, and it didn't work, so you're starting over because you got in too deep.

We're not advocating that as Black people we go out and file bankruptcy. Rather, we are saying when you've done your best, managed your finances as well as you could, and circumstances get beyond your control, there is a way to move forward. It's a way of failing forward so you can succeed in the long run.

We are not taught how to start over, but there are ways to do it. Still, it's not for the faint at heart. Without building up faith and having a plan, it's not something you can stomach well.

We were able to recover. It took hard work and diligence with our finances and the business, but we recovered.

Within a year, we rebuilt our credit, got a car, and even opened a second store. And every year since we have opened a new store or at least had one in the works.

Learning how the system works means knowing how to leverage income, finances, and businesses to maximize taxation. Clint learned early how the system worked and built on it. Now, using what he already knew and what we learned together, we consult people in business based on our experiences.

Clint learned early how the system worked and built on it.

We know strategies because we've done them. Most people don't want to experience what we did – including filing bankruptcy.

Our pastor says, "A man with experience will never be at the feet of a man with a theory." Listening to wise counsel like this is the start of you conquering your finances and mastering how they work for you.

Each time we've had to deal with a difficult financial situation, we shifted to a different level. For example, we shifted from the store insurance back to the county insurance. We transitioned based on where we were and what we needed to do. We put on different hats and changed roles from learning to fry chicken to doing social work or consulting people in business. Whether being suited up in the morning for business dealings or in jeans and polos in the evening for a night at Wingstop, we knew how to move to the level where we were needed most.

Through it all, whatever would relieve the pressure off either of us, the other would do it. That's how deep our

Marriage Retreat in Ventura
sponsored by Greater Harvest
Christian Center of Bakersfield,
CA. November 2017

love goes and how strong the faith walk had to be. Finances and faith must go hand in hand; however, it doesn't hurt to have a formula to get your finances on track.

We suggest the five Cs of finance to ensure you're headed down the right path to being prepared for any business venture.

1. **Character**

   Do you have a sound character? Can you be trusted with the money or keys to the business? You must have a good character so people know you won't embezzle or commingle funds. This means holding yourself on a higher pedestal or platform.

2. **Credit**

   This is the next aspect of preparing yourself to be businessworthy. You won't get a loan unless you show you can be trusted with money. Have you paid other people on time? Are you responsible? Do you have the resources or are you leveraged out? Franchisors look at your finances too – even if you can buy the franchise. They want to make sure you're in an excellent position to keep it going.

3. **Capital**

   Capital is the money it takes to fund what you want to get involved in. Clint knew what we needed on paper and was able to cash out some properties to have the money on hand for our purchase. Do your due diligence and understand what's needed. Of course, using other people's money is a smart way to go, but it must be leveraged wisely. If there isn't a return to pay on this money then it won't make sense for someone to give you cash. We were able to leverage our home with equity. The lender said he would invest in a lien on the property. We never missed a payment or payroll. That kept our capital standing high. We may have missed some other things but the landlord and employees never knew we were having a hard time.

4. **Collateral**

   Collateral is what you use when you don't necessarily have the capital on hand. We had our properties as collateral and believed in the business so much we could use it to leverage raising the money for the loan we needed for the business.

5. **Capacity**

   Capacity is the final "C" in the financial package. It refers to the resources you have to do the job. What does your resume look like? Once we had certification through the four-week training with Wingstop, we showed that we could be successful. The banks extended their resources/capital because of the certification in the specific field. We didn't come from a restaurant cooking background (even though we could cook), so we wanted certification for proof.

The five Cs for financial competency can help you prepare to own a business. Can you show you are able to run a business professionally? Have you done it before? These questions will help you decide if a franchise is a right fit for you. With a franchise, the expertise is in the model. You can fit yourself into what the plan says. If you maintain a minimum standard for what you do, follow the rules, and inspect how you're doing, you will meet the criteria and acquire the franchise of your dreams.

A popular question is where can you get the money to start a business. Usually, if you don't have the funds, you can get an SBA loan with maybe 10 percent down. If you have the down payment and the four other "Cs," you may be able to borrow the difference. You can also finance a business through savings, retirement funds, or inherited money.

Now, we talk a lot about franchises because we favor them. In these types of businesses, lenders let you borrow with a little skin in the game. Other models are scrutinized because there's no proven return of success. Having high marks in all the "Cs" will help you get the funding and resources you need. If you can do that, you can own a franchise. Clint has people sit with him to figure out how to get the "Cs" lined up. We love working with people on this. It's necessary. We want to help you get it together to be better prepared for the world of franchising.

Where can you get the money to start a business?

You see, from the time we decided to look into investing, we knew a franchise was for us. We were given the steps and knew exactly what we needed to be approved. There's no guesswork, so you can position yourself to win. When someone comes to us and says they want to do a franchise, we can sit with them and say what is required. We researched for over a year on how to invest and in what. We knew we wanted a business, but we did the research before jumping into anything. Most people don't want to take the time, and they don't have the patience. However, there are simple steps that must be taken. It may not happen overnight, but you can do it. You must check off the boxes and do what it takes.

What are the boxes? Start preparing yourself with the steps in the "Process" section following this chapter.

SCRIPTURES

At the end of every seven years you must cancel debts. This is how it is to be done: Every creditor shall cancel any loan they have made to a fellow Israelite. They shall not require payment from anyone among their own people, because the Lord's time for canceling debts has been proclaimed. (Deuteronomy 15:1-2 NIV)

A feast is made for laughter, and wine maketh merry: but money answereth all things. (Ecclesiastes 10:19)

The blessing of the Lord, it maketh rich, and he addeth no sorrow with it. (Proverbs 10:22)

But seek ye first the kingdom of God, and his righteousness; and all these things shall be added unto you.
(Matthew 6:33)

PROCESS

When talking about money, the rubber meets the road. Couples must learn to discuss money matters and confront money issues head-on. Part of that is knowing where you stand financially.

1. Figure out where you are financially and write a spending plan.
2. Once you understand where you stand, work on the steps to move you to where you want to be.

NOTE: The amount of money you have does not determine where you are in life. You can move to where you want to be using the techniques below. Follow these three steps to shift into your next gear for success:

a. **Measure your money:** Everything starts with knowing where you are and where you want to go. What's coming in and going out? This extends to time, attention, and money – measure for treasure.

b. **Commit to conduct:** You must have a code by which you live, which includes reliability and consistency. Conduct is a measure of character, and you must shift your character to be disciplined with diligence. Set goals and targets; take advice and report your progress until positive cash flow becomes a habit.

c. **Do your duty:** Passion, love, and philanthropy are great concepts; however, now is the time to work on saving you! As they say on flights, put on your mask, first, before trying to help someone else. Without a disciplined sense of duty, bigger than you, continuing down the wrong path is inevitable. Your duty may include taking care of the kids or the elderly. It may be hitting the workforce with your best energy every day – focused and determined. You must do your duty to move up the ladder of success.

THE BIRTH OF OUR FRANCHISE

Lesson 5

Now you know a bit about DeAnna and Clint. You know we're human, have had some good times, and we have weathered some tumultuous storms. We are everyday people just like you! We managed to come through our challenges, learn, and understand how to operate successful businesses. Now we're ready to share what we've learned with each of you. To be very clear, we are not finished learning. We still seek counsel. We still attend workshops, conferences, and training. We still listen, watch, and mostly, pray. And we still get our business grind on every day.

The franchise business is how we decided to operate as a couple. As you can see from the previous chapters, it took us a while to get where we are. Though the journey is a long one and comes with its challenges, it is attainable. You can do this! We want to help you have the success you desire if it's in the franchise world.

This chapter is about how we birthed into Wingstop's franchise world. It's time to get into the nitty-gritty. Right now, we will usually share as one voice, even though some aspects still share our individual perspectives. Face it. Clint is the straight shooter with no chaser while I may try to

55

soften it up a bit and offer a little sugar at the end of the hard lesson. With both of us, you will get an honest direction on how to be successful in this franchise world.

Franchising is a way to have a business with a brand behind it already.

First, let's understand better what a franchise is and what it's not. A franchise is a business opportunity. It allows the franchisee (the person buying in or running the business) to start a business by legally using someone else's expertise, ideas, and processes (the franchisor). Franchising is a way to have a business with a history and a brand behind it already. If this sounds rewarding and too good to be true, then you are getting a better understanding of what franchising is. Take, for example, McDonald's. Though it can be gratifying, it's not a quick and easy way to make millions. Each franchise is its own start-up enterprise although the branding and processes are already there.

Once you pay your fee, you get a franchisor license. The license gives you access to the know-how of the franchise, as well as its intellectual property to use the business model and brand. In using the features of the franchise, the franchisee must comply with the obligations set in the agreement. Then the franchisee can sell the branded products and services in their own business.

As a franchisee, you become a part of a network but not an equal partner. The franchisor still owns the rights to its brand and property; you are leasing the right to use it. Having a franchise is a growth strategy, not just for the franchisor but franchisees can grow their businesses by having multiple branches. Still, remember, franchises are temporary business investments you rent or lease. It is not a business purchase with full ownership. There is a finite term to license the business, even if you keep it for your lifetime.

HOW MUCH DOES IT COST?

A franchise can be exclusive or nonexclusive in terms of territories. That means you may have to stay in a certain area to operate or you may have open areas of operation. There are three important payments you must make to a franchisor:

1. Royalties for the trademark
2. Reimbursement for the training and advisory services
3. Percentage of the individual business unit sales

These fees may be paid individually or under what's called a single management fee. Other fees that might be included are starting fees, also called front-end fees. A disclosure fee may be one of these types of fees.

The lifetime or term of owning a franchise is usually fixed, but the fees often vary and can be broken into shorter periods or longer terms. Agreements can last from five to thirty years. Stiff penalties may be applied when breaking these agreements. All franchise opportunities differ. New models are redefining success every day. Therefore, it's hard to say what the cost is to start a franchise.

In general, you can count on fees averaging from 7% and up. Your fee can assure a geographical area and other specifics depending on what's negotiated. Also, there's no guarantee on revenues or profit, even if it's listed in the franchise disclosure document. There is no law that requires an estimate of profitability. It all depends on how much the franchisee works the franchise model. This is why franchisor fees are typically based on gross revenues from sales and not on profits.

Money can't be the main factor in your decision to franchise.

You must have your net worth in order when preparing for a franchise financially. Let's take the example of qualifying for a Wingstop franchise today. You must have a minimum net worth of $1,200,000.00 in which $600,000.00 must be liquid. To date, there's also a three-store minimum requirement to develop. Money can't be the main factor in your decision to franchise or not; however, it is something you must take into consideration.

WHAT FRANCHISE SHOULD YOU CHOOSE?

Choosing a franchise is very much an individual preference. But it's also important to remove the emotions from the decision to ensure you are in a business you can really stick with. There are several ways to decide on a franchise. In fact, these days, there are even franchise brokers who help people find the appropriate franchise. These brokers are like middlemen, helping potential franchisees narrow down their choices in the growing world of franchises.

Brokers try to match your budget and skill sets with franchises or brands for your consideration as an investment. They receive a commission from the franchisor for bringing you on board. If you decide to use a broker, take care that they are looking out for your best interest, not their paycheck. Franchisors can pay hefty commissions to get brokers to bring people their way, even if you don't fit the profile for that brand.

Having been in business as entrepreneurs before we decided to launch into the franchise world, we understood our skill sets and business. We also knew that if we were going to get a franchise, it had to be something we liked. Our first step was to talk it out. As a couple, if you are thinking of getting a franchise and you are reading this book, you must both be on the same page with your decisions. One person can't be all in and the other on the fence. It's hard work to do any business but owning a franchise is no joke. It takes everyone involved (especially in marriage) to do the due diligence necessary for the right fit.

We first examined what would be required of us and the business no matter which franchise we got. Then we talked about what we wanted out of it and why we would even consider getting a franchise. Now, here's where you really get to rely on each other in a relationship. Each of you has your unique gifts. Lean on those gifts and make them work for you!

The main two areas Clint knew were critical: credit and finance. I knew Clint was astute in those areas because he was making money in that business arena for a long time. So I followed his lead and guidance and that became our area of priority – getting our credit and finance to a stellar space. Not only is Clint the credit and finance guy, but he is also the salesperson in the family. We used his reasoning

behind sales as part of our formula to assess how we would choose a franchise. This theory included three things:
1. Would we buy the product?
2. Could we sell it to our mommas?
3. Would it enhance people and how they felt?

We decided if it passed those three, it would go on the consideration list.

DeAnna is the research queen, and that's where I leaned on her to get into what the franchise was about. She is a people person and could find information on a more personal level, not just doing internet or corporate research. DeAnna was the ideal person to find out if people would buy it, if our mommas would like it, and whether it really enhanced or made people feel good.

LOCATION, LOCATION, LOCATION

Another consideration for us was the location. We wanted a place that would work for us. A Wingstop was already in Long Beach where we lived. We loved it and ordered from there all the time. DeAnna was from Bakersfield, though, and when we were there, we had no Wingstop to order from. Seriously, we were driving around Bakersfield one night at about 10:30 and couldn't find anything to eat. Most places closed at 10:00 PM.

We decided that Bakersfield might be a good location. Again, here's where leaning on each other and trusting each person brings a gift to the table is important. Bakersfield was a great place to bring a food concept. However, it is a close-knit, small, country-type town. They don't like outsiders to come in and think they can make money off them (people from LA or down south are considered outsiders). But if there's a person from Bakersfield, they will support them. Of course, we had to let the town know DeAnna was from Bakersfield and a true local. Bakersfield High School and the Drillers were held in high esteem like alumni hold USC. Seriously, people come back from the 1950s to support the Drillers! Once we announced DeAnna was a Driller – doors opened.

It took both of us to make this thing happen. Clint managed the financial logistics and I handled the research and people. There's no way Clint could have gotten into Bakersfield on his own; the people wouldn't have embraced him. There's no way I could have done all the credit and finance work alone; it wasn't my lane. We did it together.

Now, we would have support from the Bakersfield community, but we still had to bring a brand no one really knew about there. At that time, Wingstop wasn't a household name. It was a little fast-food chain without a large following. We were the seventh store in all of California, so you can imagine this store would be very, very new to Bakersfield. No one knew who we were, and we were trying to introduce a new concept of making an appetizer the main course into an open market.

Finding our location in Bakersfield wasn't a problem. We found the perfect spot. Securing it was another story. Even after we decided which franchise we wanted and were ready to get the location, the landlords were skeptical. We're not sure if it's because they didn't really know the brand or because we were African-Americans inquiring about a substantial lease. They were not quick to accept our offer to lease. They called the corporate office to verify we were a franchisee for another space. Was the call warranted? Perhaps, but in the end, we were able to build on a space in a different location, not owned by him. Now, the original landlord who called corporate on us has asked us several times to lease space at other sites (sigh). That transaction took us a year. We took a piece of land that was initially an Albertson's grocery store parking lot and built it up from the dirt.

Do your homework and make sure that area will work for you.

The key thing to remember here is location is important. Bakersfield didn't have many food options when we opened; that made it a prime spot for us. Do your homework on the industry and the franchise you want. Some of that will be done for you. Most franchise opportunities offer a map of their locations and what is available. Even if a franchise offers you a specified location, it's up to you to do your homework and make sure that area will work for you.

We lived in Long Beach, so had DeAnna not been from Bakersfield and had family there, it may not have been the best spot for us. We had to take a lot of things into consideration before determining Bakersfield was the spot. However, after we discussed the options and talked with our business representative at Wingstop, we were convinced Bakersfield was ideal. Even when there was a downturn in the market, we held on tight to that location. It was important to us, not just because it was our flagship store but because we had some history in Bakersfield. Thus, we wanted it to succeed for the city, as well as for our personal development and growth. Choose a location that works for you.

KEEP IT SIMPLE

There are a lot of factors to consider when choosing a franchise. First and foremost, it's important to know what industry you want to be in. After looking at and researching a slew of franchises, we decided we were going to be in the food business. In the late 1990s, there were not a lot of food spots in Bakersfield, so we looked at Subway, Jamba Juice, Quiznos, McDonald's, and Burger King. We told you the story of how we were driving around looking for food and didn't find any, so that was a void that we figured we could fill – at least in the Bakersfield area. However, we hadn't considered Wingstop when we drove around Bakersfield because we never saw a Wingstop there, so the idea wasn't apparent. Then, one day, we were having a social event at our house, and it hit us. Our decision was based on being major customers. Every time we did a mixer or other social events with our family, we would order from Wingstop. The light bulb went off as we were enjoying their food at one of our social gatherings and we decided they should be part of our considerations of possible franchise opportunities. DeAnna got to researching, and the next thing you knew, we were flying to Texas to do our due diligence.

Finding simplicity for us meant looking at the menu and seeing how simple it was. We looked at a lot of menus. If something is hard to understand, and you're the customer, imagine what your potential customers will experience. We looked at things from both sides: as the seller and customer. As the customer, we didn't like being confused. As the seller, we didn't want to have an overwhelming amount of food to prepare that confused us.

Simplicity is about looking for a proven model. Franchises offer a model that works; you just need to examine whether you can fit into that working model. How the model works is a different thing. Some models may not be as simple or easy as others depending on the business you get into. We have heard of people going into all types of franchises from muffler and oil changes to window washing and paint. Whatever the model, you must be okay with how it presents itself.

The processes and steps you must go through to operate

Simplicity is about looking for a proven model.

effectively are important. Make sure you're willing to do what it takes through the franchising processes to be successful. You may be able to tweak some things but for the most part, the franchise has its methodology. Follow it.

In short, a good franchise has a cookie-cutter process. This component is key to keeping it simple.

If the franchise cannot show you a model that can be replicated the same way repeatedly, then you may want to reconsider purchasing that franchise.

To be successful, you will have to follow their game plan. Hopefully, it's a plan that was created for success, and you'll have plenty of examples to prove that it works. This is the beauty of the franchise system – it's simple. You get a ready-made plan and if you follow the benchmarks, you will meet success at varying levels. The key is following what has worked before.

Finally, our "simple" just meant finding something we wanted to be a part of and something we liked to do. We knew we liked good food; however, we hadn't thought about how much we liked preparing good food. When we thought of how we entertained and the satisfaction we received from hosting others with good food, we knew Wingstop would be a good fit. Their food was good, and we used it to entertain.

Another factor we considered was how easy it would be to duplicate the first store. Yes, we looked into the future before even purchasing the store. This was important to us. We wanted to have a clear plan and path for branching out should we desire to do so. Wingstop gave us that. They had an operational manual with all the processes. We didn't have to create that for ourselves or our employees. This again made it simple for us to build the business. It meant we could focus on the actual work of the business, instead of the administrative and operating plan.

You get a ready-made plan and if you follow the benchmarks, you will meet success.

Once we put our theory of three to task, visited Texas, did our location check, and all the other due diligence required, we were ready to buy. Looking at it firsthand, Clint came back and made sure we were a fit for the application. Due diligence, though long and detailed, is also a simple factor that puts you at the top of the game. In this case, we were in a position of power ready to buy a franchise.

You see, we planned and prepared to be franchise owners before buying a franchise. At the point where we were visiting franchises to see what they had to offer, we

had already put our financials, credit, and ideas for locations in place. We just needed to choose the franchise we
wanted to purchase. The way we investigated and vetted
the franchises was so impressive, it made the franchisors
want to work with us even more. When we flew to their
headquarters to inquire about them, we had legitimate
questions and concerns. They knew we were serious, and
they saw a concerted effort with both of us engaged. Doing
all that preparation, we could choose whatever we wanted.

So we chose Wingstop. It met our three-part criteria,
was simple, had great processes in place, and a full support
system. Most importantly, we felt as if God was sending
it to us because we had never actively sought to own a
Wingstop. The location, the newness of the opportunity,
and how everything lined up just felt right.

We had prepared and decided on the venture. We were
ready – and we were not ready! When we launched with
Wingstop, we really didn't know anything about being in
the restaurant business. This was a totally new business
and industry for both of us. There were no restaurants in
our background – except going out and enjoying the food.
How in the world were we going to own and operate a
restaurant? We decided to let God handle that like we did
so many times before when uncertainty lurked. On bended
knees, we said our prayers and began to learn what it
would take to run a restaurant, in particular, a Wingstop.

SCRIPTURES

*Suppose one of you wants to build a tower. Won't
you first sit down and estimate the cost to see if you
have enough money to complete it? For if you lay the*

foundation and are not able to finish it, everyone who sees it will ridicule you, saying, 'This person began to build and wasn't able to finish.' (Luke 14:28-30 NIV)

So if you have not been trustworthy in handling worldly wealth, who will trust you with true riches?
(Luke 16:11 NIV)

And the Lord answered me, and said, Write the vision, and make it plain upon tables, that he may run that readeth it. For the vision is yet for an appointed time, but at the end it shall speak, and not lie: though it tarry, wait for it; because it will surely come, it will not tarry.
(Habakkuk 2:2-3)

PROCESS

Now is the time to start thinking about the business you want to be in. What "floats your boat"? Is there something you can agree on that would be fun to work on together? Figure out what you want to do together that may be profitable for you.

In the previous chapter, we discussed finances. It's time to start researching what a business will cost you and figure out how you will position yourself to be ready for what you want.

AFTER THE DOORS ARE OPEN

Lesson 6

Running any kind of business is hard work. When most people are going home after their 9-to-5 jobs, entrepreneurs are revving up for the next part of their day – even if that means it's nighttime. It takes a lot of energy and determination.

Determination is about sticking to it. To be determined, you must believe in something so much you are compelled to do it. Believing in what you're doing is the first step to realizing your dream of owning and running a successful franchise. For us, it didn't hit suddenly. We suspect that's the way it is for most business owners and operators. It's a slow progression. If it's booming the first week, that's just the hype of it all. Be ready for the slowdown because those times do happen. Actually, slow periods are okay. If you are determined to make something work, you're all in.

This is one reason why we like the owner-operator business model. You must be committed to it and work at it. We're okay with that. Working in the business is where the spark of God blesses our efforts. Having the vision to buy Wingstop, being led to Bakersfield, and finding a great location were all blessings. Next came the work of the blessing.

Wingstop was (and still is) a lot of work. However, they provided the best support system a new franchise owner could have to get started. The opportunity offered everything from finding and assuring the right location with their dedicated real estate team during the site selection process to working with the construction team to secure the general contractor for the build-out process.

Our location was a huge gamble because there was nothing in Bakersfield. We believed the city really needed something, but the city could have proved us wrong. Quite frankly, they tried to prove us wrong when our business was going under and people weren't buying. We had no idea we were going to have to build the building. Not only that, we would need to create the *need* for our product. The location we chose required that we not only retrofit a building for a Wingstop, but we also had to retrofit and convince the community they needed the model.

We could have gone to LA, but Bakersfield didn't have a lot there, and it was DeAnna's home. As much as we were sick of Bakersfield, we were also in love with it and there was a need. We let the city know their country girl was returning home. Clint would literally tell people, "My wife is a hometown girl." That made a difference.

After some scrutiny, the landlords were ready to lease the building to us, but we still had to retrofit the inside to be a Wingstop. That meant it had to be built to suit. Wingstop construction provided insight and helped us make sure we complied to get up and running.

Over the years, we've learned every aspect of real estate and the construction of a restaurant. From getting space to gutting it into what's needed, we know. We do everything: installing gas lines, plumbing for bathrooms, ceilings, gas ventilation, and HVAC. To date, we've built eight restaurants and have one under construction at the time of writing this book. In 2020, we will have nine restaurants in our career portfolio – not just Wingstop but Fatburgers too. We began to understand the restaurant format because Wingstop requires multi-franchise units. We worked on the LA County and Bakersfield stores pretty much simultaneously.

As mentioned, we felt good about Bakersfield because whenever we were there to see family (Dee's mom, grandmother, cousins, and others), we looked for restaurants and there was nothing besides McDonald's and Wienerschnitzel. After we built Wingstop, other restaurants started opening. They didn't exist in 2004 and 2005. Initially, it was as if we opened a restaurant in the middle of the desert (like outside of Vegas) that no one knew. We were paving the way to start a whole new concept in unchartered territory.

At the time we opened the restaurant, one thing was sure: Wingstop had prepared us with efficient tools to run their model. The training was top notch. We spent time at their support center in Dallas, Texas, for four weeks learning all the ins and outs of the business. The training was comprehensive and showed how a proven model could work. It also provided certification in the business. Certification or proof of expertise goes a long way with banks and creditors. It confirms you know what you're doing in your field of interest.

> **Wingstop had prepared us with efficient tools to run their model.**

In any business you own and operate, you should *be an expert* in your craft and have pride in your work. We believe you must also be hands-on to be successful. Most successful people who are self-made really know the intricacies of their business. They know what they're doing. In our business, we refuse to let anyone else know more about what we do than us. This means we constantly educate ourselves about franchising and the food industry. This type of interest requires a passion for what you're into. An example is the ranch dressing we serve. The ranch comes as a side, and it costs more. What most people don't know is we make these dressings every day from scratch. So when someone asks why it costs more, we can say why. Once you make fifty pounds of ranch, whipping your arms into shape, you can explain why!

Wingstop gave that hands-on type of training we needed before we put it into practice. It also teaches you that "All money ain't good money," so we stay in our lane and remain focused. The training included everything from knowing the proprietary recipes for the flavors of wings to dealing with the health department and ensuring permits and certifications are in place. Even though our concept was similar to many fast-food restaurants – throwing the chicken into some grease to fry – it was still a method to the madness of Wingstop, in particular. With the training from Wingstop, we were ahead of the curve for opening other franchises. For instance, when we decided to get into Fatburger, some things were universal to the food business like dealing with the health department; these concepts were across the board.

After choosing the location, building it out, and getting trained in every aspect imaginable in the business, Wingstop expects you to get to the business of running the business. We can pretty much assure you this will be the case with any franchise. Once you've paid your dues in money and training, it's time to get busy.

With Wingstop, even when it's time for you to run the business, you're still not alone. They provide ongoing operational and marketing support from their teams who have seen everything from quick start-ups to snail's pace businesses. Whenever there is a question about the business, we have an account manager we can go to. This type of support and training is something we recommend you look for when evaluating the franchise of your choice.

Once our training was done and the location opened, it was time to get busy operating Wingstop. That's exactly what we did. In the first few years, we did okay – even with our obscurity. However, the third year during the recession things got tough! We had to close the Whittier restaurant. Quite frankly, the Whittier store wasn't in a good location; we didn't know that at the time, but we know now. Location, location, location is very important.

Fatburger Bakersfield Grand Opening located next door to our 2nd Wingstop location in Bakersfield. September 2019

KNOW YOUR WHY

When some people see you start a project, they want to jump on the bandwagon. This is exactly what happened when we ventured into our Wingstop enterprise. However, we let them know we had to do intense research and base our goals around training, as well as our ultimate wants and needs. Equally important was knowing our "why" before we started.

Deeply rooted principles are the basis for any authentic "why."

Knowing your "why" is significant because it leads you to "what" you will be doing and "how" you will be doing it. If your "why" is all about making money, then our concepts and way of doing things may not work for you. We base our "why" around intangible things. We also believe that deeply rooted principles are the basis for any authentic "why." Our "why" begins with living in and following the footsteps of Christ. With that as our foundation, we focus on family, legacy, and life enjoyment. Knowing what we wanted, we established long-term goals and then applied the "what" and "how" to get there.

We decided to work with a food establishment. The rest of the decisions revolved around the type of food and how we wanted to operate. We didn't know anything about running a restaurant, but we weren't oblivious. Wingstop was going to get our money, so we could sell a product to someone else. This product happened to appeal to a market of those between the ages of eighteen to thirty-five, which is a great customer base to have. It was simple. Remember one of our first rules was to keep it simple. We wanted a simple menu. We didn't want to deal with a full-service restaurant. These factors may seem small, but they were huge in our decision-making process. You must know your "why" and what you're willing to do to get to it in order to have a successful business. This is even more important when operating a business as a couple. You must have a unified response.

We have friends who looked into a franchise that was a bit more complicated but cheaper to invest in. This couple put their money into a franchise opportunity without having everything in order. When they couldn't fulfill the location requirement of the franchise, they lost their initial investment, which was substantial. The point to this is, their hearts weren't in it, so it became more challenging to find what they needed and how they would operate. It ended up not happening at all. Just because it's within your budget doesn't mean you should do it. Again, your "why" should be more than money. Passion for your endeavor is crucial.

Establishing the "why" helped us choose how we would operate. An example of how the operation differed from a normal Wingstop was we purposely chose not to sell alcohol. We did this even though, at the time, Wingstop required that you sell alcohol. It's a Dallas-based company, and they're used to having wings and beer. In fact, they ask that you sell everything that's on their menu. We negotiated out of that option because it wasn't a part of our value system. This was not something that happened immediately. We proved ourselves to be viable and of value. Over time, as our business grew, they knew we were legitimate operators and allowed us not to have alcohol.

Our "why" also involved bringing other people in, as well as helping develop and grow a segment of the population many people often forget about. We opened the business to employ those who may not be given a chance otherwise – the unemployable. Typically, these are people who end up having poverty or survival issues even though most are good, solid folks. Unfortunately, in many cases, they make poor decisions because of their involvement in the wrong circles or a cycle of bad things happening in their environment. Finding steady employment can shift the cycle. It can be the difference between living on the streets and having a roof over their heads. But the cycle isn't broken that easily in the type of jobs we offer. We can only give them a start and consistent income.

We promote from within, all the way up to district manager.

Still, childcare, transportation, and health care are realities that can throw even the best employee off. However, we work with our employees assuring them when something comes up, they still have their jobs. On top of working with our employees in their current positions, we also promote from within, up the ladder all the way to district manager. It's not likely you'll be a manager with us if you are not already employed in a different position in our company. Of course, when we first started, we hired all the way up to manager. We work people up from the bottom.

Edy, our longest-standing employee, has been with us for twelve years starting about a year after we opened. He is now the manager of two locations. He commutes back and forth just like we did over the years. He has always had two jobs even before working for us. Prior to us, he had an oil change job; then he came into the restaurant business with us. He was an English language learner, so it was difficult at first, but he stuck with it, and we stuck with him. He even enrolled in night school to become proficient in English. Now after the consistent training we've provided, he can run circles around most of the employees. Our district manager, James, has been with us for ten years now.

Our employees don't do anything we are not willing to do, so they must be passionate about the business too. We are "all in" with what we do, so we train people to do what's needed.

Our "why" is all about people, giving and fulfilling our God-given purpose. Sharing our experiences through this book is not a new venture. The objective is to help you take a step toward fulfilling your God-given purpose. When you take one step toward God's plan for you, He will take two steps with you. Our steps have been rewarding in ways we never could have imagined. They were challenging too! In the next chapter, you'll learn a little about how we grew from envisioning one Wingstop to having multiple franchises. Once the doors are open, the flood gates await!

SCRIPTURES

But he that knew not, and did commit things worthy of stripes, shall be beaten with few stripes. For unto whomsoever much is given, of him shall be much required: and to whom men have committed much, of him they will ask the more. (Luke 12:48)

His lord said unto him, Well done, thou good and faithful servant: thou hast been faithful over a few things, I will make thee ruler over many things: enter thou into the joy of thy lord. (Matthew 25:21)

For even when we were with you, we gave you this rule: 'The one who is unwilling to work shall not eat.'
(2 Thessalonians 3:10 NIV)

PROCESS

1. What is your "why"?
2. How do you satisfy your yearning to fulfill it?
3. Have you started researching the business you want to pursue?
4. What does it look like?
5. Chart out a plan or map of how you see the business you desire.

MULTI-UNIT FRANCHISES

Lesson 7

Business is all in the numbers. That's a fact. So having Clint, probably the most effective "bean counter" you'll ever meet, is a major asset. Clint puts processes and systems together. Plus, he's good at blue-collar work. He got the building construction gene from his father's side of the family and had a chance to work on the Superdome. He's not afraid of getting calluses to get the work done. However, his schooling and calculating brain have kept him from getting deep into the construction aspect.

On the other hand, I love working with people. This quality is invaluable because human capital is one of the most important components of operating a franchise. When owners are not available, the people who have been hired must be able to step up and do the work that needs to be done.

Together as a dynamic duo, we brought Wingstop Los Angeles and Bakersfield to life in 2006. Having no idea of the debt we would eventually carry or that our store would end up being a multimillion-dollar business, we operated the way small business franchise owners do – we worked. Who would have guessed the number of wings we'd sell in the city?

Fatburger Glendora Grand Opening, May 2019

Wingstop Stockdale Grand Opening. July 2019

Wingstop Stockdale before picture. June 2018

Today, we have five Wingstops and four Fatburger restaurants. All the Wingstop chains are in Bakersfield, while the Fatburger restaurants are spread out in Bakersfield, Glendora/Monrovia, Arizona State campus in

Wingstop Stockdale Grand Opening. July 2019

Tempe, and one in Barstow off the 15 freeway.

Moving into a new chain of restaurants was easier than beginning the work with Wingstop. We used the same formula to go into Fatburger that we used for Wingstop. Again, we used our simplistic theory of three:

1. Would we buy it?
2. Could we sell it to our mommas?
3. Would it enhance people and how they felt?

Looking for something we were interested in and found value in seemed to resonate with food. Fatburger was an establishment we frequented for years. We loved their products. Most important, it was a simple concept. Instead of wings and fries, we were getting into burgers and fries.

We owned a Wingstop for six years on Oswell Street in Bakersfield, having grown the business since the beginning. We did great with that location, so we figured that would be a great place to have a Fatburger too.

An example of how well we did with the Wingstop: during our first year in that location, we missed the million-dollar mark by only $10,000 or less. But the second year, we blew it away. It's now an over two-million-dollar store. We grew the business from an average store to being the top performer in the entire franchise. Shortly after opening in that location, there was a suite next door with a dental office. Those offices were closed and the suite was vacant for about five years. We talked about finding something that would fit into that spot, so when Fatburger came to our attention, we jumped on it.

When you're on the right track with God's plan, things just fall into place. Sure, obstacles come up. We had many challenges during our years but when it's right for you, it just works.

We grew the business from an average store to being the top performer.

We sent an email to Fatburger to discuss the possibility of taking on a franchise, and they began talking to us. Our representative was the director of the franchise. On one call, we mentioned having a location in Bakersfield. He went silent. The pause made us think he didn't understand what we saw in the location. That was okay. We knew people didn't see what we saw. Furthermore, they didn't know the plans God had for us. We were ready to explain. But just as we were about to speak, we heard him chuckle. Now that we know him better, we are sure he was grinning. With his chuckle, he explained he was born and raised in Bakersfield and went to high school on the street we were suggesting. He said he'd been looking to put something there for the past two years. With that, we told him his problem was solved, and we closed the deal to get that territory. It was one of the few signals that we were doing the right thing at the right time. Now, this director calls us just about every other day with locations.

Each location we have acquired over the years has been a blessing. Barstow was an already existing location turned over from a foreign national when a manager stole all the equipment. We ended up getting a good deal on this location. Then, the Glendora branch was an opportunity because the landlord was trying to get rid of a teriyaki spot that was underperforming. It was a great deal because the numbers made sense. It was a good location. The landlord was amenable to breaking the lease and letting us in. We kept some equipment and construction costs were lower than starting from scratch. Finally, we had initially acquired the Arizona space with a french fry concept in our head – French Fry Heaven. We researched this concept while looking to get into something new. However, we shut this idea down quickly because it was problematic. Fatburger was a better prospect.

Getting into these businesses was more than just a monetary investment. We work the business. That means effectively running operations, improving employee morale, ensuring the right locations are right, construction is complete, and everything else that goes with operating a business.

People ask how we juggle all of these at the same time.

1. First, we stuck with the same industry when expanding. This means the basics stay the same. What's hot and what's cold stays the same.

2. Our focus is on the cleanliness of the store, customer service, and quality food products. These things transfer from one restaurant concept to the next. Much of what we do is common sense. Once you learn the ropes with one food service industry business, it's not difficult to take it to another.

3. The biggest thing for us was choosing a simple format we could commit to. We didn't choose a Subway or McDonald's because their concepts had too many variables and things to do. It wasn't simple enough for us. Our biggest variety with Wingstop is the sauces. All the chicken goes in the same. With Fatburger, it's just flipping burgers. You must keep the meat separate and there's a stacking order (poultry or dairy versus veggies). Those are internal food safety rules that involve food storage and preparation standards.

Get certified to ensure you know the ropes.

Most things are the same in the food service industry. You get certified to ensure you know the ropes. The standards are pretty much the same once you learn the food industry. That makes it a lot easier to run multiple franchises. Temperatures are usually the same across the board with what degree hot or cold should be. First in and first out are also the same across the board. How you store and cook food is generic to meet health standards. For example, everything in the fridge is at 40 degrees below or if cooked, 165 degrees internal temperature is used or it can't be served. The main difference is the product you sell and the brand. We say "the Wingstop way" because it gets personal when you look at the brand and how they do it. We like how Wingstop sets up its training and operations.

Running multiple franchises can be very lucrative. However, it's important to get your first venture underway and operating successfully before jumping into additional prospects. We had success in our first franchise before exploring the next. Success for us means being able to meet payroll and include ourselves on the list.

Find your level of success and make it happen so you can decide if multiple franchises are right for you.

SCRIPTURE

His master replied, 'Well done, good and faithful servant! You have been faithful with a few things; I will put you in charge of many things. Come and share your master's happiness!' (Matthew 25:21 NIV)

PROCESS

Look at the map/plan you've created for your business. Does it include multiple ventures? If not, consider doing a mind map of how it might grow. It helps to have a flip chart or graph paper for this exercise.

Place the business idea in the center of the graph paper and put a circle around the idea. From that point, brainstorm around ideas that might expand or grow from your business idea. Draw a line from the center circle to an outer circle, creating branches from the original idea.

As you plot these ideas, you will continue to expand your thought process. This will provide new ways in which you can make your business a reality.

FAMILY AND FRANCHISE

No matter what we do, we put God first. Family is right amid our worship with God. Family is our priority from our past, present, and future. When thinking of family and the business, our ancestors are our inspiration as much as our children. Future generations are our aspirations. In all of them, we seek to glorify God's name.

How does the food franchise industry relate to family and our spirituality? Well, we can date it back to when Clint traveled to Paris with his French class. At age seventeen, he cooked bulk dinners to raise the money to go. His family is from New Orleans so cooking Creole style and in bulk is in his blood. As a family, we all cook because we like to eat.

Every step of the way, we count on our families to help us when asked. When life got rough before the franchises and while we had them, our families were always there to step in. On one occasion, we had vacancies at a

When life got rough, our families were always there to step in.

*Family birthday picture. Center – Marie Daniel-Sturdivant,
l-r – Christian Shears, DeAnna, Clint, Cydni, Beverly Daniel-Nichols,
Rosalie Lewis, Jenene Shears, Daniel Shears.
Back Row l-r Alvin Lewis, Clarence Watkins, CJ, and
Charli. November 2018*

store and didn't have sufficient staff. We were hiring people on the spot and putting them on the line to work immediately. In the interim, our kids, nieces, and nephews were working shifts. It was all hands on deck. They came through until we could hire fifteen to twenty people to keep us going.

Dee and I have learned to count on each other. We play off one another when it comes to getting the work done. If one of us must go to the store,

Christmas Vacation at Big Bear Mountain, CA l-r Alexis Kemp, Cydni, Torri Guyton, Vicki Kemp, DeAnna, Kennedy Schaffer. Christmas 2018

the other can take care of the kids. We depend on each other. As said earlier, money is the source of most marital breakups. However, God has preserved us. It seemed as if when we had the money woes, we came together more. We would present the situation and figure out a solution.

Even when Clint made decisions I had doubts about (like when we got all these houses), we still stuck together. When it was good, it was good, and when it crumbled, we had to figure it out. If the stores were falling apart, there was no way we would make it if we fell apart too. We stuck it out.

Family Vacation in Cancun Mexico – l-r Kennedy Schaffer, Taylor, Tasha Dobson, Cydni, Kevin Dobson Jr., CJ, Tiffany Dobson, Kevin Dobson Sr., Tamara Dobson, DeAnna, Clint, sitting Kelsey Schaffer, Angel Schaffer, Dennis Schaffer. August 2014

Driving the kids back and forth to keep the stores open was part of the day's events. We did all that as a family. Those were the times we had the longest conversations. Money – or the lack thereof – showed us how to unite as a family. Not that we ever want to live through some of those tough times again, but we know we can get through anything as a family.

Clint never missed a day seeing the kids and family when we were really in the grind. He would set up the morning shift,

Cydni's junior year at San Jose State University. She is the power forward for the women's basketball team. September 2019

go to his regular work in finance, pick up the kids from school, have dinner with us, and then do a night shift. At times, he would sleep in a motel so he could open the store in Bakersfield only to take the two-hour drive back home to see the kids in the morning. Technically, the kids didn't know he wasn't home at night. As a mom and wife, I was happy he had set a routine to ensure our family stayed together.

Picnic at Morehouse College with CJ. August 2016

Our children grew up in our entrepreneurial world. As preteens, they worked in the restaurant and would get paid too! They would do homework at the store and sometimes a tutor would come in to help them finish. Once they were done, they could help until it was time to close the store. Then we would drive back home. They spent many days on Wingstop benches and tables.

My niece, Charli's middle school graduation from Intellectual Virtues Academy in Long Beach, CA with Principal Jacquie Bryant. May 2018

The blessing of our children is that they were always giving and compassionate. Even as the business became successful, they never got "big-headed." We're sure everyone says this about their children, but our kids are great! That includes my niece, Charli Southall, who has been with us since she was nine.

We never had problems with them cutting up and acting out. We raised them to be balanced. No matter what was going on, we did the same things as always. Whether it was a plane trip or a

Our 2014 Christmas Card with Charli, CJ, and Cydni

Family time was instilled as a value.

road trip, we spent time together. These were the things we thought were important. Family time was instilled as a value. We never purchased designer clothing or items for our kids. We felt introducing them to superficial things might make them less appreciative of things that had intangible value. Training your children to be the people you want them to be is challenging but doable. The Bible says we should train our children in the way we want them to go (Proverbs 22:6).

One disturbing thing for us as parents was finding out our compassionate and loving children had experienced bullying. Our son, CJ, shared with us recently that because he didn't have designer clothing and the like he was bullied. He said he wished he had some of the designer shoes and clothes so the kids wouldn't have picked on him. We were devastated because we felt he could have told us about anything. Obviously, he felt he couldn't. None of our children ever asked for expensive tennis shoes or name brands because they wore school uniforms K-12. We were shocked to learn he was bullied. Our kids obviously were not aware of what we had or they didn't want to brag about it. Either way, it didn't feel good to have our son talk about being bullied.

When it comes to family, we focus on faith. We walk by faith and not by sight, so everything is intertwined with the Lord to be pleasing and acceptable in His sight. Put the family first with God at the head, and you'll never go wrong.

SCRIPTURES

For we walk by faith, not by sight. (2 Corinthians 5:7)

The Lord will make you the head, not the tail. If you pay attention to the commands of the Lord your God that I give you this day and carefully follow them, you will always be at the top, never at the bottom.

(Deuteronomy 28:13 NIV)

But seek first his kingdom and his righteousness, and all these things will be given to you as well. Therefore do not worry about tomorrow, for tomorrow will worry about itself. Each day has enough trouble of its own.

(Matthew 6:33-34 NIV)

PROCESS

It's time to do some reflection and assessment.

1. How is the process going?
2. Is entrepreneurship or entering the franchise world a real prospect for you? If so, what are you willing to sacrifice to enter this business world and determine if it's worth it?

As a couple, you must talk about these things. Family is too important to let anything distract you from its tenets. Figure out ways to put family first, and you'll be on the way to your dream.

CHALLENGES OVERCOME

Lesson 9

I, DeAnna, was a doubter. Even when life was good, I would think something bad might happen. As challenges continued to come our way, I began to learn to relax more, understanding God had plans for us in our lives. Everything we do is God's purpose for us as we set an example here on the earth. I think there's something for everyone like that.

Unfortunately, we don't always live up to it, but there's a purpose for us. As I walk in that purpose, I want to know God is pleased with me. I stopped worrying about things I had no control over. For example, it makes no sense for me to worry about hiring a construction person or contractor. I can't do the job, so I must figure out how to get a builder to do it or hire someone else. As I learn to deal with stress and problems, even when losing money, I'm learning to trust in God for everything. It's a faith walk and spiritual growth for me.

CLINT

Gaining from the experience of the Lord bringing me through in the past makes me feel more confident I can do something again. I always look at the goal. Whatever the ultimate blessing or devastation, I look at it and ask: what's the worst that could happen? Once I take that perspective, I feel okay with it and work backward. Now, nothing that happens is a shock because I've already accepted it. If I can live with the worst, whatever happens, it is normally better. I certainly can live with that. This helps me keep moving. It's part of my faith walk because I have the peace of acceptance. It's funny because, without the expectation of the Lord coming for personal rapture, everyone wants to be in the grace of the Lord, but no one wants to die. When you know the grave is not the end of the story, you are confident no challenge is insurmountable. I apply these principles to every aspect of my daily walk. When it gets overwhelming, I comfort myself with thoughts like these. I truly believe once you live in the moment and let go by letting God, the quicker things start turning around for you.

Trust your partner, even when life throws doubt your way.

We are coming to the end of the book, so we thought we would share those opening thoughts that identify a little more about our personalities as individuals and how we work together – walking by faith. The opening quotes of "the doubter" and the "faith walk" are appropriate in many areas of life. In relationships, you must trust your partner, even when life throws doubt your way. Still, doubts mean intuition is kicking in; that's something to pay attention to as well.

There's a reason to be a doubter and to have a strong faith walk when working as a couple in the restaurant franchise industry. This stuff is not easy. As much as we like to keep things simple, there's still a lot to manage. What we've been through, quite frankly, might break a couple if they don't have a spiritual connection with God.

Dee's favored line was, "Are we painting or packing?" It meant we were either sitting still or moving in some sort of way. Our lives have been filled with feast or famine. Because Clint never had a regular paycheck (being an entrepreneur and often, on commission) everything was about performance. As much as we relied on his earning potential, we also began relying on the Lord early. Clint was always there – as early as the age of eighteen. However, I had to really pray and learn my faith walk. God never failed us monetarily. Remembering that helped us keep it together and strengthened our faith.

Normally, when finances are together and expectations are pretty much met, everything else can be fine-tuned. But when the financial storms start raging, you can imagine how off-kilter the world can get. In our case, you can guess who wasn't affected by our down cycles so much and who thought the apocalypse was coming! Having each other to lean on helped us feel we would be okay. Having God on our side, we knew we would be okay.

By the time Dee got into the painting or packing groove, she had learned to weather the storms. It was a lesson in allowing God to take care of the family in other situations. By that time, we realized God had done it in the past (blessing us beyond belief in the worst of times), so we knew He could do it again.

We also recognized we couldn't change anything – not an hour to a day. We couldn't add an inch to our stature (Matthew 6:27). We just had to go back to Scripture and give no thought for tomorrow (Matthew 6:25). We knew and trusted that God cares about the sparrows in the sky, and He surely cared about us.

I constantly rehearsed that Scripture and had to pray. I talked to God, telling Him I didn't know what to do. He told me to relax. I also had to learn to stop begging in my prayers. When you are always begging God to give you something in your prayers and then you realize it's the worst thing you could ask for, you don't want to be on the receiving end. Maturing in faith means you know if it's for you, it's going to happen. We must do our part because faith without works is dead, but when you put your best foot forward, God will meet you with your needs.

Clint and I have excellent work habits, and we're committed to our projects. So we know that the rest will fall in place or perhaps it was something we weren't supposed to do anyway. It doesn't mean we don't feel hurt, but we get through and sometimes realize when something didn't go through, it was something we escaped. We don't have control. We don't even decide on waking up in the morning. Life has shown us this through the loss of family and friends – reminders that we have no control. It doesn't mean we should not prepare and do things. Rather, we must prepare and make wise decisions knowing God is in control.

We made it through tough times. One store closed and another was slowing with the economic crash. We downsized, gave up cars, and handled business like we needed to. We had a Mercedes and a Lexus; one of them had to go. The Lexus was almost paid off, so we said good-bye to the Mercedes S550. When they came to repossess it, the guy couldn't believe how easily we opened the gate, handed over the keys, and let him take it away. He said he was surprised because he wasn't used to being welcomed in to repo a car. As far as we were concerned, it wasn't worth giving up peace in our family for something that wasn't working for us.

Owning a franchise and nice cars didn't matter if it was draining our energy and spirit. This was where Clint's faith helped me overcome my fears. Who cares that you have Wingstops and cars if you're losing everything? Clint had to help me with that. My faith was fleeting, but he had enough to help me. Now that we have had to lose some things and literally rebuild, I know what it feels like. I can handle it. I have faith. If Clint told me right now, "Babe, we gotta shut down and start over." I'd say, "Okay, what's our next move? Painting or packing?"

There's never really a sacrifice because we're led spiritually in what we do. We were looking for an investment to use our cash flow when we began the franchise business. We knew the real estate market wasn't going to be sustainable all the time, so with Clint's financial advisor hat on, we began positioning ourselves to diversify. That was Spirit-led. When the real estate bubble burst, we had already diversified.

Granted, we had no idea how long the economy would bleed. No one could anticipate that everything would dry up, but we knew a change was coming. And, if you had told us we would be upside down for over six years, there's no way we would have agreed with you! Nevertheless, our faith made us persevere. We

Times were tight and tough, but we weathered the storm.

never folded. The register was still ringing in 2008 – not as much – but it was still ringing. Hanging in there meant figuring out what we could keep and what had to go. Even when Dee had to go back to work for the county, we never gave up. Our not getting paid didn't mean we didn't make payroll. No matter what, we made payroll for those we had committed to. We rode it out. Times were tight and tough, but we weathered the storm.

We are committed to our faith, and with that, we're steadfast to each other. We want people to see us sticking to our convictions fully. We are not so quick to throw in the towel. We are the "wait and see" couple. Most people give up because they don't see the endgame. They don't know the business and economic side of it. We literally had people coming into our Wingstop to sneak and take pictures as if they could build a better "wing trap." Little did they know their answers were as easy as asking us a question. We aspire for others to be successful and would share the formula or "the game" as so many call it. We share information to keep others from making the same mistakes. Having already lost a franchise, we can share what that's like. We can give the same lessons we're sharing in this book. We are spiritual people who want to help other God-fearing people move forward.

We follow what our pastor taught: plan for the next thirty years but live like you're going to get out of here tomorrow. That's what living through a faith walk is like. We have grown through our business, spirituality, and faith as a couple. Now take some time and reflect on how you can use your spiritual growth to get through the challenges in your life.

SCRIPTURES

The Lord is my light and my salvation – whom shall I fear? The Lord is the stronghold of my life – of whom should I be afraid? (Psalm 27:1)

I can do all things through Christ which strengtheneth me. (Philippians 4:13)

Trust in the Lord with all thine heart; and lean not unto thine own understanding. In all thy ways acknowledge him, and he shall direct thy paths. (Proverbs 3:5-6)

PROCESS

1. Starting a business can be a heady proposition. It takes time to understand what arena you want to work in. It also takes a strong commitment to make sacrifices.
2. Take some time to reflect on what you must sacrifice to make your business work.
3. Choose five Scriptures each that you will hold to when challenged and in times of trouble.
4. Share your Scriptures with each other and confirm you will agree with the Scripture for each other.

JOY UNSPEAKABLE

Lesson 10

We've taken you on a journey of how we started our business and given you some steps on how you might consider your own. The "Process" sections in the book are designed to get you working on an implementation plan. Along our business journey, we've had some challenges and good times. Following are some stories that make us laugh, feel happy, and just give us joy when we think back on them. They are stories of courage and conviction, snippets of some of the challenges we faced and some of the good times we enjoyed after getting through those challenges. We hope these stories will give you a glimpse of what it's like to "own your own" – the good, the bad, the ugly, and the joy of being "boss bosses."

FROM RAIN TO RAINBOW

During 2008, the economy was going downhill, so were our business revenues. Determined to stay in business, Dee went back to work and I manned the store as often as possible. We closed the Los Angeles store to save the Bakersfield location. There was so little income coming in we had to figure out how we would pay to keep the doors open. This meant some of our vendors were not paid on time.

One such vendor was a towel company providing toilet paper. Yep, we couldn't afford to pay for sheets to wipe booties! The towel company representing our paper goods came in and literally repossessed the toilet paper, paper towels, and dispensers. Imagine how surprised we were to have a company come in and take our paper goods! There was no way we would let that stop us, so we headed to Rite Aid, got some supplies, and kept going.

We asked for forgiveness for the half-truth we told a new paper vendor the next day. We called and said we were unhappy with our other company (which we were) and wanted to set up a new vendor account (which we did). New dispensers were installed. A new account gave us some leeway to make the payment and keep the new vendor from having to shut us down.

Speaking of being shut down, we had contractors and vendors suing us left and right as we tried to keep our heads above water. The U.S. Marshals came into the restaurant to shut down the credit machines for tax issues. This meant

With every challenge of rain, we looked for the rainbow.

we could only take cash payments. Not only did the Marshals shut the machines down, but they also sat around waiting for the cash payments to come, so they could collect! You see, as soon as we gathered a couple of hundred dollars in the register, we would have to turn it over to the Marshals. They would stand with a bag and "tap your till" as they called it.

These are just a few of our hardship stories. Yet, in spite of it all, we kept our heads held high. Our goal was to stay the course even though it was getting more and more difficult. We just couldn't give up. With every challenge of rain, we looked for the rainbow. In the end, our survival was that gift.

RUNNING THE BUSINESSES

We take turns working on various parts of the business, but no matter what, we keep the balls juggling. Whether it's building schedules or making payroll, one of us handles the business of the business. It can be challenging but at the end of the day, we see how the business is running and that gives us unspeakable joy to know we are actually "doing the thang!" Some of the areas you will have to deal with in most any business include the following:

1. Creating schedules
2. Payroll
3. Bookkeeping
4. Maintaining proper inventory
5. Purchasing
6. Customer service
7. Personnel services (hiring, training, termination, etc.)

Having the experience of running a restaurant is, by far, one of the best training experiences ever. As mentioned before, our pastor and counsel says, "A man with experience will never be at the feet of a man with a theory." We believe this is true and enjoy the training we get from Wingstop and Fatburger. The experience we have allows us to look at our wins and losses and build on the foundation we've started. When we fail, we know we can try again and succeed because we have already experienced failure.

THE PEOPLE ARE THE POWER

The biggest headache and most rewarding thing in our business is staffing. We hire people who leave for various reasons but return. Some start with us from the time they get their first work permit until they finish school. Others grow up with us and end up buying homes.

We've had hardworking, diligent workers and others who didn't do what they were supposed to. Some steal, and we must let them go. Others move up the chain from cashier to manager. No matter what, we invest in our employees. We know they are the heart of the business. We've always paid above minimum wage. It's a commitment we made from inception. We also pay extra fees, so we can pay our employees every Friday. That choice was made to ensure our people have the funds they need to navigate the challenges they have. Feeding our employees is important to us. We give a daily employee meal free of charge. Since we couldn't always be at the store, this removed the temptation to steal and assured our employees were not hungry.

Still, with all that we offer, we're the first ones to get calls

Human capital must always be negotiated and navigated.

and grumblings asking for a raise because minimum wage is going up. We're already paying over the minimum wage. It's kind of funny, but we love our employees.

No matter what the business, human capital must always be negotiated and navigated. Some take their jobs seriously and want to do better; others don't care. We want to help people learn life skills and are successful with some noteworthy employees. Once we let our employees know we want to help them, and we're willing to train and teach them, it's up to them to accept the challenge. We let them know when they stick with us and show great character, they can grow with us. We plan on growing big. We want people to be successful.

One thing we knew from the start is if you don't pour into the people you hire, you can lose them. We enjoy our staff, and they know it. When hiring, we search for people who will fit into the culture we've created. They buy into the vision we see for our stores. With the right mentality, they can grow with the business and become like family. Our employees know our stores and mission are bigger than us because we are community-minded and accept our social responsibility. We do giveaways and scholarships. It's more than just selling chicken or burgers. We uplift those around us.

Most workers don't see how much it costs to run a business like this or how to maintain our vision. We train and ingrain the points into our team, letting them know the business is not about working to take care of our family but our community. If employees think they are working only to take care of the boss, they will feel they have a license to steal. Our environment is one where no one must feel the need to steal.

STEALING IN THE NAME OF STUPID

I'm good with people and know them well. Hence, Clint lets me do the training, while he keeps the operations and business setup going. Basically, our crew knows us as Momma Bear, DeAnna, and the stern but fair Poppa

Bear, Clint. We bounce off each other to keep the business running but when it comes to the people – that's me. Many times, I take it personally when my team doesn't do what they're supposed to do. Clint keeps telling me it's just business, but it still hurts.

We had an employee steal from us after we'd given him money on several occasions for medicine, rent, and all sorts of things. We couldn't understand why he did it. Of course, he lost his job, and we prosecuted him. It ended up being a bad situation for him. As much as we wanted to keep helping him, we had to pursue the case because he'd left one store where he was the manager and had access to the other stores. He went to one of the other stores and stole the money. Had we not tracked it properly, we would have been blaming the other manager for the theft. It seemed like he was trying to set up the other manager. Shame on him! In the end, he had to pay restitution and got some time. We didn't follow it closely, but we did have him arrested at the store so others could see. Setting an example was important for us. Again, we didn't understand this employee as he walked right into the store, knew where the cameras were, and stole from the register. This wasn't the only theft we had but it was a show of the world's stupidest criminal!

On another occasion, one of our biggest disappointments was a young lady we had supported time and time again. When people ask for help, we usually give it. This young lady needed help burying her mother. We helped her only to find out she was stealing from the stores. When we had to let her go, it was heart-wrenching. She tried to deny it until finally, she broke down and apologized. What could we do? We had to let her go.

Most of the people we hire no one else will. People would come and go, even employees who were not so good. In the old days, we'd give everyone a second chance – and a third! Now, we draw the line. We let our employees know if they want to be part of our culture, they must do the right thing. And they do!

One young man worked with us on the weekends and attended school studying electrical engineering. He was diligent even when he was a cook with us. From day one, we knew he would be successful because he had discipline and a good work ethic. We want people like this to maximize their potential.

There's a lot we do for our employees as business owners that goes above and beyond the call of duty. Our employees are young, many times uneducated, and barely surviving. It's tough for them, so we strive to give them a better chance. When they're willing to work hard and listen, they can grow into leadership with us. We've always been givers and that works for us. When things don't go as they should, whistleblowers let us know before it gets out of hand. We believe our employees know we have open hearts; that's why we don't have a lot of theft or stupidity.

LEADING BY EXAMPLE AND EXCITING MOMENTS

We see many successful people in this industry who are just telling people what to do instead of doing it themselves alongside their employees. Regularly, we show up in full uniform for opening, closing, or even working during busy times.

Super Bowl weekend is a perfect example. We committed a year in advance to work all day on Super Bowl Sunday. All hands had to be on deck for one of our busiest days of the year. Super Bowl Sunday brings two and a half to three days' worth of business through the door. When we're in the store, we're not eating chicken and shouting out orders. No, we're shoulder to shoulder with the employees making sure the orders are completed for customers.

I still enjoy getting on the line and calling out the orders, too. Clint doesn't mind doing it, but as he says, "I'm not one to say I enjoy it. I did the business as a business, so I expect it to do well or I'll close it. I do love that we are helping employees."

When we are part of their success, we feel great.

Being there with our employees helps us know them better. When we are part of their success, we feel great. Recently, an employee who started with us long ago returned to tell us he had purchased a home. We were excited because we had been part of helping him move into management. He left us and came back just as strong as ever. He has done well after having his first job with us. Now we get to see the other side of how we impact people's lives.

That people see us as positive figures – able to give them direction, guidance, or advice along the way – is a bonus. Whether we have served as personal or professional role models for them, we feel successful because they are moving in a positive direction. It goes the same for the community.

Recently, we received the award for Entrepreneur of the Year in Bakersfield. We were over the moon. It was out of the blue! We had no idea as no one even mentioned we were in the running. This great surprise had us so excited.

We have so many tentacles in the community, and people ask us questions all the time, but we didn't expect to be honored for it. We love being a part of the positive things happening in the community and in people's lives. When we can be guiding lights to others, we are there to do it.

Getting acknowledged for our work is a good feeling, but I like seeing Dee excited as she gets her personal business accolades going with writing and speaking. She's getting her due. Her transformation is exciting to me.

Clint is pretty competitive. He said years ago he wanted to be the highest tither in the church. We're doing our part. After thirty years, I'm not sure if he's gotten there, but, collectively, he's probably there because he's so consistent. That's a personal trophy he wears that gets him most excited out of all the accolades he has received from sales and other things. Tithing gets Clint fired up.

We received recognition from our community, the employees, of course, from our heavenly Father and – after attending six conventions – our industry. We really had started to wonder where our favor was in the industry. Yes, we had financial success, but it seemed we always missed the mark when it came to being recognized at the business level with Wingstop. One year, we sat at our table and didn't even mind that our backs were to the stage. We figured a Texas team would get the awards for the night, and we would walk away empty-handed as usual. When they called our names, you would have thought we had won a Grammy. The excitement was overwhelming. It was our first corporate-level recognition at the annual convention. What a fantastic experience! The award was for the highest sales increase. The trophy was a golden goose. Now, we have a few of those but that first one felt incredible. Every year we're recognized for something these days. Mostly, it is in sales and new store openings.

The longevity of being together as a solid couple doing business is thrilling. We're still around and one of the youngest couples to have a franchise. We're perhaps the only Black restaurant owners in Bakersfield, and we're thriving.

Awards for top sales in Wingstop brand. We have received this recognition every year since and more. Three of our Wingstop Bakersfield locations are in the Top 25 of over 1,200 restaurants nationwide

But these days, most of our joy comes through service. We just had our third annual turkey giveaway and gave complete meals to 250 families. We also give food to local schools, backpack giveaways, and a scholarship to Greater Harvest Christian Center in Bakersfield annually. Philanthropy is a whole new way of thrill-seeking. Before, we were excited just to keep the doors open and make sure our employees were paid and cared for. Now, it's about being able to give back on top of that.

Unspeakable joy is about hitting the pavement and giving the best during the tough times. It's about training, sharing, and leading in the community. It involves working with and loving people. It's how we work our business and stay positive no matter what comes our way. And, mostly, it's about serving God and always walking in the path He has prepared for us. We get to

wear the boss shirts because we've stepped up, worshipped, glorified, and recognized the real boss – Jesus Christ, our Savior. Do you want to wear a boss shirt? Work your purpose-filled life and boss up!

2nd Annual Wingstop Bakersfield Turkey Giveaway held at GHCC Bakersfield, CA. November 2018

SCRIPTURES

> *Be joyful in hope, patient in affliction, faithful in prayer.*
> (Romans 12:12 NIV)

> *A cheerful heart is good medicine, but a crushed spirit dries up the bones.* (Proverbs 17:22)

> *For I know the plans I have for you, plans to prosper you and not to harm you, plans to give you hope and a future.* (Jeremiah 29:11 NIV)

PROCESS

1. Think about one of the toughest times you've experienced in your relationship. Share your feelings with each other about it. Find the silver lining and feel the joy from the storm.
2. Make a list of the top ten worst things that could happen in your business venture. Now write the remedies, solutions, or consequences of those things. Once you know the worst of the worst, you can let go of the fear.

SUMMARY

Lesson 11

That's it. This is the last lesson of the book. We hope you learned something from our ups and downs. In this lesson, we'll give you our final tips and one last "Process" section for you to work on before going off to launch your business venture.

You can do this! Any business you set your mind to, you can make it happen. And if you can keep your doors open, even at a bare minimum with people still enjoying the product (service, cleanliness of establishment), you can make it. Customers want that personal touch, so be there for them. We were there by choice and by force (sometimes it was just us), but we were there. Customers began to like us because they saw us there. Familiarity breeds family in the case of business. The more people see you working your business and trying, the more they will like you. Sometimes our customers see us and comment, "They got the big dogs in tonight." We respond, "Somebody's gotta do it!"

We work with the crowd and work in the lobby. People tell us stories of how they brought their kids in and remembered when we first started. They keep coming and multiplying, bringing in other family members as they grow. We love that we have customers who have stayed with us through the tough and great times. It's another reason we give back a lot to the community.

Always thank your customers. We thank them for continuing to come and for spreading the word. You can never thank customers enough. Keep doing it.

Do your due diligence. We can't express this enough. A lot of people say they want to get into business, but they don't do the homework. We invite people to ask us for help. However, we also encourage them to do their homework before asking us. We're happy to help and want people to ask because it's painful to see them ignore what we've been through and then make the same mistakes or worse. People want to talk about business. Now, we need you to be about it.

Understand your customers. We found that people between the ages of eighteen to thirty-five were a great win with Wingstop. Find the customers that match your business, and you'll know how to create a winning formula too.

Business is an active process. It's not as easy as opening and then resting on your laurels. There's passive and active income, but business is an active participatory investment that you must put action into. What's good about being in business is that most of the time, people don't have money to do passive investments. Business is an investment in trading work for money. Robert Kiyosaki talks about a four-quadrant principle to be a success. Everyone in America fits into one of those positions:

1. Employee
2. Self-employed
3. Business owner
4. Investor (having their money work for them)

THE CASHFLOW QUADRANT
LINEAR INCOME VS RESIDUAL INCOME

YOU HAVE A JOB
TIME = $
NO LEVERAGE
E EMPLOYEE

YOU OWN A SYSTEM + PEOPLE WORK FOR YOU
PEOPLE = $$$
LEVERAGE
B BUSINESS OWNER

YOU OWN A JOB
TIME = $$
NO LEVERAGE
S SELF EMPLOYED

MONEY WORKS FOR YOU
$$$ = $$$$$$
PASSIVE INCOME
I INVESTOR

Robert Kiyosaki® from his book "Cash Flow Quadrant"

Learning nuggets of wisdom from greats like Robert Kiyosaki, Napoleon Hill, and our pastor, gives us a lot to chew on. When you're fed good meat, it governs your life and how you live. Fortunately, we received those good nuggets early. That helped govern our lives. We gleaned from the experiences we were exposed to. That saved us from bad decisions and mistakes – even though we also learned from the same things. Get some advisors and mentors and save yourself a lot of frustration. You will learn from them.

Get some advisors and mentors and save yourself a lot of frustration.

We are happy to serve as mentors through our lessons. Our final lesson in the "Process" section includes "wisdom nuggets" we gathered over the years. Use them to launch to your next level. Turn your thoughts into communication and your communication into action. We wish you the best in everything you do and look forward to hearing how you build Faith, Family, and Franchise to create your best success.

SCRIPTURES

Let the wise listen and add to their learning, and let the discerning get guidance. (Proverbs 1:5 NIV)

The heart of the discerning acquires knowledge, for the ears of the wise seek it out. (Proverbs 18:15 NIV)

The fear of the Lord is the beginning of knowledge, but fools despise wisdom and instruction. (Proverbs 1:7 NIV)

PROCESS

Use the wisdom nuggets in the next chapter as a guide to create your own. We provided eighteen nuggets, so why don't you aim for twenty!

WISDOM NUGGETS

Lesson 12

1. Never loan someone more than you can give them. This way, if it doesn't come back, you haven't lost. If you can't give it, don't loan it. We have a lot of benevolence out and still love and hug those people just the same.
2. A man with experience will never be at the feet of a man with a theory.
3. Don't talk about it – be about it.
4. Don't look at other people's relationships; work within your own. Work with the best helpmate for you.
5. Kids are very different, so you must deal with them as unique individuals. Figure out how to deal with each distinct personality.
6. Keep up with your own accounting. Never get so busy or big that you don't know what's going in and out. Celebrities and athletes have shown us this over the years when they go bankrupt or get in trouble with the IRS.
7. Know the numbers and what should be done.
8. Have checks and balances with reports, etc.
9. Use technology to do multiple things and automate.
10. Put reliable and responsible people in place.

11. Use equity (strategic) partners or people who are vested in the project, so everyone has skin in the game.
12. Our strategic partners get skin in the game doing the business just like us.
13. Take a chance on people and believe in them until they show you they can't be believed in.
14. Treat your people like you want your family to be treated.
15. Model yourself the way you want your people to be.
16. All hands on deck means all hands (including the kids).
17. Plan for the future but live like there's no tomorrow.
18. Pray.

SCRIPTURES

Wisdom is the principal thing; therefore get wisdom.

Wisdom is the principal thing; therefore get wisdom: and with all thy getting get understanding. (Proverbs 4:7)

The one who gets wisdom loves life; the one who cherishes understanding will soon prosper. (Proverbs 19:8 NIV)

For the Lord gives wisdom; from his mouth come knowledge and understanding.
(Proverbs 2:6 NIV)

OUR PRAYERS

Lesson 13

In the restaurant, our biggest prayer is that if anyone takes something, let it not be a life.

Pray for the spirit of discernment to recognize the intentions of others and to know whether to deal with them or not.

We pray for favor with people because we interact with vendors and others who can open doors for us: landlords, other professionals, financiers/bankers. We pray for their health and well-being.

Pray for strength, health, and the catalyst to keep your mind intact.

Pray for humility. Let us stay humble enough to keep doing what we're doing and be blessings to someone else.

Pray to never let us get beside ourselves by being arrogant or haughty.

We are constantly praying to remain humble yet not letting others disrespect that we are who we are. We pray to understand how to be a successful business couple.

We pray to always watch our words and let the meditation of our hearts, as well as the words of our mouths, be acceptable to God.

Pray to be an example to others so they can succeed.

Pray to let people get it out before we have to slam and go there.

Pray that we enjoy the comforts of now.

Pray to be an example to others so they can succeed. We pray that people can see us as an authentic, complete woman and man of God like the graphic tees that say, "billionaire couple" but without the arrogance.

SCRIPTURES

The Lord makes firm the steps of the one who delights in him; though he may stumble, he will not fall, for the Lord upholds him with his hand. (Psalm 37:23-24 NIV)

Keep this Book of the Law always on your lips; meditate on it day and night, so that you may be careful to do everything written in it. Then you will be prosperous and successful. (Joshua 1:8 NIV)

CLOSING

We talked yesterday about planning for next year and ate lunch for almost four hours just talking and enjoying each other. Setting goals keeps us together. We discussed challenges we're still going through and each of you reading this book. We hope the journey we shared has sparked a fire in you to begin an extraordinary journey of your own. Please write to us and tell us about it!

ACKNOWLEDGMENTS

This book is dedicated to our children Clinton Lewis Jr. and Cydni Lewis, also to our niece Charli Southall, nephews Daniel and Christian Shears and Robert Southall IV. In loving memory of my grandparents Emory and Geneva Daniel. May we forever be your examples.

To all who call us Uncle and Auntie, thank you for the motivation and force that keep us striving to do and be better because we know you are all watching. We love y'all for real.

Thanks to our parents, Papa Alvin, Mom Mom Rosie, Nana Mickey and Papa Clarence, the biggest supporters and loudest cheerleaders a couple could ever have. You are the best grandparents; our children are blessed to have you.

To our sisters, Pamela Lewis and Jenene Shears, you two are our first best friends who witnessed us first hand evolve into who we are as individuals and as a couple. Being raised in the house with us you understand all the quirkiness about our personalities. You love us unconditionally and it does our hearts good to hear our children call you Auntie Pam and Auntie Pebbles. To our brother

Charles, you were in the grind with us at the birth of our first Wingstop and we will never forget you. Love you.

To our family, thanks for constantly reminding us of our roots and who our greatest supporters are, so we will never forget.

The brotherhood and sisterhood are like no other. We are bonded for life. Thank you for every hug and tear, the sorrow, joy, laughter, and each emotion we've experienced together. Thank you for every time we had breakfast, lunch, and dinner, for every trip we've taken – from Embassy Suites with free breakfast to Four Seasons and Ritz Carlton. The times we've spent together are priceless. You are the best table talk crew anyone would be lucky to sit with. To God be the glory for what He has done for us. We love y'all for our lifetime.

Bishop Howard A. Swancy, you have been the best pastor and father in the gospel. We are so blessed as a young and now older couple to sit under your leadership. Your guidance is unmatched. We love our Peace Apostolic Church family.

> *How, then, can they call on the one they have not believed in? And how can they believe in the one of whom they have not heard? And how can they hear without someone preaching to them? And how can anyone preach unless they are sent? As it is written: 'How beautiful are the feet of those who bring good news!'* (Romans 10:14-15 NIV)

Bishop Vernon and Lady Vicki Kemp, our prayer partners – thank you for answering every call we've made to you and asking if we need help before we could finish saying hello. Thank you for debunking the myth that we have everything and need nothing. My Shug, I really appreciate the daily reminders: "Finish the book, girl" (LOL). We appreciate and love you dearly. Your support is God sent.

To our author mentors Chantaye E. Brown and Thyonne Gordon, this entire project began because you were both convinced that my husband and I have a story to share. Thank you for the encouragement and advice you gave throughout this 5-year journey to completing our story. We love you both dearly.

Kimberly Stewart and Christian Living Books, you were and are a Godsend to us to assist us with the completion of the book journey. After the first phone interview with you, the idea of self-publishing was thrown out the window from the top floor. I found someone more picky than me:-) Your professionalism, guidance, patience, keeping us on track and attention to detail was the icing on the cake for us. You brought our journey to life and we are so grateful.

Thank you so much for your support!

To Gervel Sampson Photography, thank you for the awesome photoshoot for the cover and About the Authors photographs. Your work is second to none.

Thanks to all who know us and everyone we know; you have a special place in our hearts. We see and love you.

ABOUT THE AUTHORS

Clint and DeAnna Lewis are the owners of five Wingstop and four Fatburger franchises. Since opening their first Wingstop in July 2006, they have received numerous corporate awards including the Million Dollar Store Club and the Top Sales Increase Stores awards. Together, this couple brings a wealth of experience, education, business talent, and dedication to the fore as they help people find balance with faith, family, and finances.

Clint and DeAnna have been married for 22 years. They have raised three amazing children: their son and daughter Clinton, Jr. and Cydni who are in college, as well as their niece, Charli.

For over 30 years, DeAnna and Clint have been proud members of Peace Apostolic Church in Carson and Greater Harvest Christian Center in Bakersfield.

Clint is also the managing partner and co-founder of Felton & Lewis Financial Group, which merged into what's now Generational Wealth Inc. He has over 25 years of financial consulting experience and expertise in financial planning, wealth management, organizing client portfolios, business consulting, and valuations. He oversees all of the firm's operational engagements and utilizes his considerable experience to guide numerous clients in their financial affairs.

Clint studied business law at Glendale Community College and continued his education at Aenon Bible College in Los Angeles where he studied theology. He also attended PFS University as a student of financial planning and became a Certified Personal Financial Analyst.

DeAnna began her career 25 years ago and is not only a successful entrepreneur but also an expert orator on teen issues, business topics, and just about everything in between. She is an excellent example for women, teens, and professionals who want to improve their families, faith, and finances.

DeAnna founded Boss Sisters Connect where empowerment cultivates bosses. She is also the co-founder of Girls Win Inc., a non-profit organization that helps girls ages 12-18 years old in the foster care system. With over 20 years of experience as a social worker, a Bachelor of Science degree in Business Management and a Master's Degree in Educational Counseling, DeAnna is qualified and determined to change lives for the better. DeAnna is also a member of Alpha Kappa Alpha Sorority, Inc., Kappa Omega Omega Chapter.

Passionate about giving back, DeAnna and Clint are actively involved in their church and community, particularly, in Bakersfield where DeAnna grew up. They are proud scholarship sponsors for Cal State University of Bakersfield and Harvest Connection Bakersfield. As part of their community outreach, they also sponsor and support several local high schools and provide complete meals for over 250 families.

CONNECT WITH US

Facebook	Faith Family Franchise
Instagram	@Faithfamilyfranchise
Twitter	faithfamilyfranchise
Email	info@faithfamilyfranchise.com (Business and Booking)
Website	FaithFamilyFranchise.com
Phone	(562) 451-5300

CPSIA information can be obtained
at www.ICGtesting.com
Printed in the USA
JSHW011509240420
5251JS00002B/5